SPEAKING OF DOGS

SPEAKING
OF DOGS

The Best Collection of Canine

Quotables Ever Compiled

DOGGEDLY ASSEMBLED BY
James Charlton

FETCHINGLY ILLUSTRATED BY
Arnold Roth

GODINE
BOSTON

First published in 2017 by
GODINE

Library of Congress Cataloging-in-Publication Data

Names: Charlton, James, 1939- editor. | Roth, Arnold, 1929- illustrator.
Title: Speaking of dogs : the best things ever said about man's best friend /   edited
by James Charlton & illustrated by Arnold Roth.
Description: Jaffrey, New Hampshire : David R. Godine – Publisher, 2017.
Identifiers: LCCN 2016050114 | ISBN 9781567925883 (alk. paper)
Subjects: LCSH: Dogs–Quotations, maxims, etc. | Dogs–Poetry. |
Dogs–Anecdotes.
Classification: LCC PN6084.D64 S695 2017 | DDC 636.7–dc23
LC record available at https://lccn.loc.gov/2016050114

Second Printing
Printed in the United States of America

∼ TABLE OF CONTENTS ∼

Introduction VII

Puppies and Their Children 1

Acquiring a Dog 6

Naming a Dog 13

Dog Food 15

Chews This, Not That 20

Dogs & Cats 23

Dogs & Women 27

Smart Dogs 31

Love & Loyalty 35

Talking with Dogs 41

Travel with Dogs 49

Man's Best Friend 53

Not Sure About Dogs 57

Barking & Biting 59

Sit. Stay. 65

Breeds 75

Those Who Work and Those Who Wait 82

Pastimes: Walking, Hiking, Hunting, Playing, Swimming 88

House Dogs 97

Dogs & Humans 102

Love a Dog 108

Dogs Are Better 114

Shows & Clothes 117

Presidents & Kings 123

Old Dogs 129

All Good Dogs Go To Heaven 134

Introduction

ABOUT FOUR YEARS AGO, my dog Homer died of cancer. He was a Great Pyrenees, a huge white mop of a dog who was totally lovable and loving. The inevitability of the loss did not lessen the pain, and indeed the death of a beloved dog has been the catalyst for many writers to channel their feelings. John Galsworthy, Jimmy Stewart, Eugene O'Neill, Lord Byron, and Anna Quindlen are just a few of the writers who published memorials to their departed pets.

I was no different. As I moped around the house after Homer's death, my wife suggested that I deal with the grief by compiling a book of quotations about dogs. After all, I had edited some half dozen books of quotations. Why not dogs? I brightened. Soon I was happily reading my way through hundreds of books about dogs: memoirs, training books, humor titles, serious tomes on the biology, anatomy, and origins of dogs. Novels. Poetry. Nothing was off limits. What emerged were hundreds and hundreds of delightful, heart-warming, insightful remarks, observations, anecdotes, and quotes about our favorite pets.

Also emerging along the way was a Great Pyrenees puppy named Cooper, our fourth. Cooper has grown from a

20-pound fur ball into a large couch-hogging, fur-shedding sweetheart of a family member.

A major part of the appeal of this book are the special illustrations by Arnold Roth. Arnie's work has earned him a place in the illustrator's Hall of Fame and his illustrations are in the permanent collections of several museums. His work is one-of-a-kind, and the humor and insights he brings to his art makes me suspect that he was a canine in his previous life.

In an 1899 New York Times book review discussing Rudyard Kipling's *The Jungle Book*, the reviewer concludes that "there is, indeed, a great deal of humanity in a dog." After reading this book, I think you'll agree.

JAMES CHARLTON
New York City

Puppies and their Children

When you feel really lousy, puppy therapy is indicated.
SARA PARETSKY, *Burn Marks*

Happiness is a warm puppy.
CHARLES M. SCHULZ, creator of *Peanuts*

The first night she cried herself to sleep, and frankly so
did I. The puppy books had warned us that the transition
would be difficult for her–She'd just spent eight weeks lying in a big pile of brothers and sisters nuzzling her mom,
after all.
MARTIN KIHN, *Bad Dog (A Love Story)*

We have not to gain his confidence or his friendship: he is
born our friend; while his eyes are still closed, already he
believes in us: even before his birth, he has given himself
to man.
MAURICE MAETERLINCK, *My Dog*

A puppy is but a dog, plus high spirits, and minus com-
mon sense.
AGNES REPPLIER, *American Austen:*
The Forgotten Writing of Agnes Repplier

Buy a pup and your money will buy
Love unflinching, that cannot lie.
Perfect passion and worship fed
By a kick in the ribs or a pat on the head.
Nevertheless it is hardly fair
To risk your heart for a dog to tear.
RUDYARD KIPLING, *The Power of the Dog*

The biggest dog has been a pup.
> Joaquin Miller, *Selected Writings of Joaquin Miller*

Whoever said you can't buy happiness forgot about
little puppies.
> Gene Hill, American outdoor writer

Oh the saddest sights
in the world of sin
Is a little lost pup
With his tail tucked in.
> Arthur Guiterman, *Little Lost Pup*

Puppies exposed to mildly stressful experiences from a
very early age (1-6 weeks) usually develop into dogs pos-
sessing superior problem-solving ability, with less emo-
tional imbalance than their counterparts raised without
such stimulation.
> The Monks of New Skete,
> *The Art of Raising a Puppy*

When a puppy takes fifty catnaps in the course of a day,
he cannot always be expected to sleep through the night.
> Albert Payson Terhune

Puppies are a pain at any price, and we marked up a lot to
exuberance. Certainly she wasn't shy. Just ask our neighbors. Many times she helped them with their groceries and
tossed in a prostate exam on the house.
> Martin Kihn, *Bad Dog (A Love Story)*

Marley was young and wired, with the attention span of algae and the volatility of nitroglycerine. He was so excitable, any interaction at all would send him into a tizzy of bounce-off-the-walls, triple-expresso exuberance.

JOHN GROGAN, *Marley and Me*

The dog was created especially for children. He is the god of frolic.

HENRY WARD BEECHER

Children and dogs are as necessary to the welfare of the country as Wall Street and the railroads.

HARRY S. TRUMAN

I suppose there is a time in practically every young boy's life when he's affected by that wonderful disease of puppy love. I don't mean the kind that a boy has for that pretty little girl that lives down the road. I mean the real kind, the kind that has four small feet and a wiggly tail, and sharp little teeth that can gnaw on a boy's finger; the kind a boy can romp and play with, even eat and sleep with.

WILSON RAWLS, *Where the Red Fern Grows*

Every puppy should have a boy.

ERMA BOMBECK

My husband and I are either going to buy a dog or have a child. We can't decide whether to ruin our carpets or ruin our lives.

RITA RUDNER

All bachelors love dogs, and we would love children just as much if they could be taught to retrieve.

P.J. O'ROURKE, *The Bachelor Home Companion*

To a dog, the baby is just another dog – and not a very good one at that. His head is way out of proportion to the rest of his body, his nose is too insignificant to have any practical value, his fur is visible only on the top of his head (if at all), his odor is not nearly as that of most dogs. The human infant strikes a dog as a breed in need of some improvement.

STEPHEN BAKER, *How to Live With a Neurotic Dog*

The fact that she was no longer the favorite in the household caused her to snap at the baby one day and bite her under the eye. This happens often, much too often, when an infant takes precedence over an old-established pet. It is a safe and highly recommended rule to follow Thurber's Law in such a situation: never bring a baby to the dog, always bring the dog to the baby.

JAMES THURBER, *Thurber's Dogs*

No symphony orchestra ever played music like a two-year-old girl laughing with a puppy.

BERN WILLIAMS

Has he bit any of the children yet? If he has, have them shot, and keep him for curiosity, to see if it was the hydrophobia.

CHARLES LAMB

Acquiring a Dog

Money will buy a pretty good dog but it won't buy the wag of his tail.

    JOSH BILLINGS, 19th century American Humorist
aka Henry Wheeler Shaw

Rule Number One: You may have as many dogs as you wish, applying the formula of one dog per acre, and since our fiefdom in its most current survey extends to only about a quarter of that landmass, I have told her repeatedly that she's already exceeded her ceiling on dogs by a factor of four. Any waiver of the rule, I argued, would be madness.

    BOB SHACOCHIS, *Dogs We Love*

The best way to get a puppy is to beg for a baby brother – and they'll settle for a puppy every time.

    WINSTON PENDLETON,
    How to Stop Worrying – Forever

No man is so poor that he can't afford to keep one dog, and I've seen them so poor that they could afford to keep three.

    JOSH BILLINGS, *Josh Billings' Sayings*

My dog ain't worth a plug nickel, but I wouldn't take a million dollars for him.

    HEATHER BUCHANAN,
    American author on her dog Casper

No matter how little money and how few possessions you own, having a dog makes you rich.

    LOUIS SABIN, *All About Dogs As Pet*

"Kay, would you like a dog?". . . Ike asked.
"Would I? Oh, General, having a dog would be heaven."
"Well," he grinned. "if you want one, we'll get one."

    KAY SUMMERSBY MORGAN, *Past Forgetting:*
    My Love Affair with Dwight D. Eisenhower

"I don't want you to be alone," he said after a while.
"I'm used to it."
"No, I want you to have a dog."

    META CARPENTER WILDE, *A Loving Gentleman:*
    The Love Story of William Faulkner and Meta Carpenter

I was a tiny kid, and my parents couldn't get me a dog, 'cause we just didn't have the money, so they got me, instead of a dog – they told me it was a dog – they got me an ant. And I didn't know any better, y'know, I thought it was a dog, I was a dumb kid. Called it 'Spot'. I trained it, y'know. Coming home late one night, Sheldon Finklestein tried to bully me. Spot was with me. And I said "Kill!", and Sheldon stepped on my dog.

WOODY ALLEN

When you adopt an animal you create a little miracle. You right a little bit of what's gone wrong on this harebrained planet of ours. You feel like every superhero rolled into one, because you took something dark and awful and made it light again.

CAROL LEIFER, *A Letter To My Dog*

I wondered if by adopting Otto, I had sealed my fate as a single woman with a dog. I could see our future together. Me and him. Otto and Julie. "Happy Holidays from Julie and Otto," accompanied by a picture of Otto dressed in a Santa hat. Well, so be it. At least I wouldn't be alone.

JULIE KLAM, *You Had Me at Woof*

For many years I thought that owners of small dogs harbored stunted souls. Parents of infant beauty queens. Weird bachelors with pet stairs by their beds. Adult hoarders of dolls and teddy bears. People deranged by an obsession with the adorable.

WELLS TOWER, "Small Dog, Big Heart."
Garden and Gun, June 2014

When I adopted him, he was a neglected slip of a thing, but his heart was capable of soaring. I call on his spirit when things get logy, when I feel an internal clock slipping into what Dickinson called an "hour of lead." Attention to the mortal shadowing of all beauty – that's a perspective that comes to me too easily, something I have to resist. And that's why I loved the heavy golden paw tapping on my knee – notice me, come back. A kind of sweet slap, with the blunt tips of his nails poking at me. A slap I miss now with all my heart.

MARK DOTY, *Dog Years*

I let her off the leash, and she circled the yard, tail down, head down, nervous. She'd been penned up for a long time. I worried she'd run away or turn nasty. We all sat and watched. Eventually, she'd completed her rounds and returned to me. She took the leash in her mouth, wagged her tail, and said with her eyes, "I am your friend. I am the one you've been looking for."

BILL HENDERSON, *All My Dogs*

No man can be condemned for owning a dog. As long as he has a dog, he has a friend; and the poorer he gets, the better friend he has.

WILL ROGERS

Like many other much-loved humans, they believed that they owned their dogs, instead of realizing that their dogs owned them.

DODIE SMITH, *The Hundred and One Dalmatians*

There are stores where dogs can be had for a price; often as many as half a dozen dogs are placed in a show window, and passersby are apt to praise them vocally in the presence of dogs who also happen to be passing by. It comes as a shock to even the most self-confident dog that he can be replaced.

STEPHEN BAKER, *How to Live With a Neurotic Dog*

Wanted: a dog that neither barks nor bites, eats broken glass and shits diamonds.

GOETHE, quoted in W.H. Auden's *A Certain World*

I bought a puppy last week in the outskirts of Boston and drove him to Maine in a rented Ford that looked like a sculpin. There had been talk in our family of getting a 'sensible dog' this time, and my wife and I had gone over the list of sensible dogs, and had even ventured once or twice into the company of sensible dogs. . . . But after a period of uncertainty and wasted motion my wife suddenly exclaimed one evening, 'Oh, let's just get a dachshund!'

E.B. WHITE, *E.B. White on Dogs*, by MARTHA WHITE

Acquiring a dog may be the only opportunity a human ever has to choose a relative.

MORDECAI SIEGAL, *A Dog For the Kids*

Acquiring a Dog

I wanted a dog to guard the Place and to be a menace to burglars and that sort of thing. And they've sent us a teddy bear.

ALBERT PAYSON TERHUNE, *The Coming of Lad*

I picked out Murphy the way I imagine a socially stunted middle-aged man might select an Eastern European mail-order bride: late at night, hopped up on processed snack food, guided only by an internet profile featuring a few grainy photos and a paragraph of personal history.

BETH KENDRICK, *Are You Smarter Than a Terrier*

I pick dogs that remind me of myself – scrappy, mutt-faced with a hint of mange. People look for a reflection of their own personalities or the person they dream of being in the eyes of an animal companion. That is the reason I sometimes look into the face of my dog Stan and see wistful sadness and existential angst, when all he is actually doing is slowly scanning the ceiling for flies.

MERRILL MARKOE

It seemed that we were people of such evident solidarity, Blackie abandoned promiscuous begging and attached himself to us as our permanent dog. His devotion was exemplary and his appetite enormous. He slept by the fireplace and he had perfect manners.

ERNEST HEMINGWAY, "The Christmas Gift"

Sam adopted me on sight. It was though he had read the Faithful Hound Manual because he was always near me; paws on the dashboard, as he gazed eagerly through the windscreen on my rounds, head resting in our bed-sitting room, trotting just behind me wherever I moved.

JAMES HERRIOT, *Favorite Dog Stories*

It is simultaneously never the right time for a new dog, no matter what, and always the right time for a new dog, no matter what. I have learned it doesn't matter what you think you are doing in your paltry human life. Put another way, the natural world is in alignment when it sends a dog your way. It may be aligned for you or against you.

GUY MARTIN, "The Urban Gun Dog," *Garden and Gun,* December 2010

There's something about a soldier and a stray dog. They belong together. Dogs prefer a pair of khaki pants and G.I. shoes to trot beside. They obviously love parades; the first notes of assembly will bring pups scurrying from every corner of the field.

COREY FORD, "Parapups"

Naming a Dog

And the Woman said, "his name is not Wild Dog anymore, but the First Friend, because he will be our friend for always and always and always."

RUDYARD KIPLING, *The Cat That Walked By Himself*

Names of dogs end up in 176th place in the list of things that amaze and fascinate me. Canine cognomens should be designed to impinge on the ears of dogs and not to amuse neighbors, tradespeople and casual visitors.

JAMES THURBER, *Thurber's Dogs*

We had called the dog Stranger out of the faint hope that he was just passing through. As it turned out, the name was most inappropriate since he stayed on for nearly a score of years, all the while biting the hands that fed him and making snide remarks about my grandmother's cooking. Eventually the name was abbreviated to "Strange," which was shorter and much more descriptive.

PATRICK MCMANUS, *A Dog For All Seasons*

My name is Chance. I know, it sounds odd, but most names do if you think about it long enough.

CHANCE, *Homeward Bound*

This is ridiculous! It's a dog, he doesn't have preferences! You could call him Ding-Dong Head and he wouldn't know the difference!

CHARLES GRODIN, in *Beethoven*

Mister, don't call that dog "Lifesaver."
No?
Call him "Shithead."
Good.
"Shithead." It's exciting. It's just exciting to have this kind of life on the road.
A guy and his dog.

STEVE MARTIN, in *The Jerk*

His name is Rufus II, but the II is silent.

WINSTON CHURCHILL, whose first poodle
was named Rufus

Dog Food

FROZEN
FOODS ⇨

I don't eat anything that a dog won't eat. Like sushi. Ever see a dog eat sushi? He just sniffs it and says, 'I don't think so.' And this is an animal that licks between its legs and sniffs fire hydrants.

    BILLIAM CORONEL

You gonna eat that?
You gonna eat that?
You gonna eat that?
I'll eat that.

    BIRCH, as dictated to Karen Shepard.
    Unleashed Poems By Writers' Dogs

Don't eat the car! Not the car! Oh, What am I yelling at you for? You're a dog!

    TOM HANKS, *Turner and Hooch*

~ 15 ~

The only food he has ever stolen has been down on a coffee table. He claims that he genuinely believed it to be a table meant for dogs.

JEAN LITTLE, *Stars Come Out Within*

I have seen a dog doing what he ought not to do, & looking ashamed of himself. Squib at Maer, used to betray himself by looking ashamed before it was known he had been on the table, – guilty conscience. – Not probable in Squib's case any direct fear.

CHARLES DARWIN, *The Descent of Man*

In typically human fashion, dog owners cling to the notion that their pets demand a special kind of nourishment. This is not true. Dog's needs are the same as human's; roast turkey will do.

STEPHEN BAKER, *How to Live With a Neurotic Dog*

Dog Food

You can always trust a dog that likes peanut butter.
KATE DiCAMILLO, *Because of Winn-Dixie*

The great thing about working with dogs is that if you show up with food you don't usually have trouble recruiting subjects. Usually. We showed up in Puerto Rico at a fishing village and the dogs turned up their noses at roast beef sandwiches. They were used to eating fish entrails.
Dr. ADAM BOYKO, *New York Times* article
on origin of dogs October 21, 2015

Ever consider what they must think of us? I mean, here we come back from a grocery store with the most amazing haul – chicken, pork, half a cow. . . they must think we're the greatest hunters on earth!
ANNE TYLER

I wouldn't convict a dog of stealing jam on circumstantial evidence alone, even if he had jam all over his nose. . . . Well behaved dogs don't eat jam.
PROFESSOR AUGUSTUS S.F.X. VAN DUSEN,
in *The Motor Boat* by Jacques Futrelle

Some of the objects he grabbed were small enough to conceal, and this especially pleased him – he seemed to think he was getting away with something. But Marley would never have made it as a poker player. When he had something to hide, he could not mask his glee.
JOHN GROGAN, *Marley and Me*

A bone to the dog is not charity. Charity is the bone shared with the dog, when you are just as hungry as the dog.

JACK LONDON

If a dog's prayers were answered, bones would fall from the sky.

ANONYMOUS

The dogs eat of the crumbs which fall from their masters' table.

MATTHEW 15:27

A dog's instinct, coupled with common sense, tells him that feeding time is all day. Man insists on giving him only one or two meals, instead of a hundred.

STEPHEN BAKER, *How to Live With a Neurotic Dog*

Every night it's the same.... I have supper in my red dish and drinking water in my yellow dish.... Tonight I think I'll have my supper yellow dish and my drinking in the water in the red dish. Life is too short not to live it up a little!

SNOOPY, *The Complete Peanuts, Vol. 8*

My pit bull was choking on his dinner: I squeezed his stomach and the neighbor's cat shot right out.

SCOTT WOOD

They have dog food for constipated dogs. If your dog is constipated, why screw up a good thing?

DAVID LETTERMAN

This was a town where a man was once not regarded as respectable unless he was accompanied by his dog. But a reform movement had set in, led by several local religionists, and gambling had been abolished and there was even a movement on foot to forbid a dog entering a public eating place with his master.

ERNEST HEMINGWAY, "The Christmas Gift"

As soon as I began to eat my lunch, all the dogs clustered close around and I distributed small morsels to each in turn. Once Jimmie, Queen and Boxer were sitting side by side, tightly wedged together. I treated them with entire impartiality; and soon Queen's feelings overcame her, and she unostentatiously but firmly bit Jimmie in the jaw. Jimmie howled tremendously and Boxer literally turned a back somersault, evidently fearing lest his turn should come next.

THEODORE ROOSEVELT, describing a hunting expedition that he took after the death of his wife and mother on the same day that his first child Alice Lee was born. *Outdoor Pastimes of An American Hunter.*

Chews This, Not That

Marley had sent more leashes and ropes to their graves than I could count; he even managed to chew his way through a rubber-coated steel cable that was advertised "as used in the airline industry."

JOHN GROGAN, *Marley and Me*

There was not much that Millie wouldn't chew. She chewed baseballs, croquet balls, basketballs, the floor mats of my car, rake handles, empty beer cans, the Tonka trucks in the sandbox, the sand box, and the sand in the sand box.

P.J. O'ROURKE

Ah, poor Fidele, what mischief thou hast done.
    Sɪʀ Isᴀᴀᴄ Nᴇᴡᴛᴏɴ, after his dog chewed up a
    manuscript containing years of calculations
    and writings.

For example, a puppy might be able to eat only the toe of
a slipper, a child might well succeed in eating the whole
shoe – which, considering the nails and everything, would
not be wise.
    Rᴏʙᴇʀᴛ Bᴇɴᴄʜʟᴇʏ, *Your Boy and His Dog*

John Steinbeck's Irish Setter puppy, Toby, chewed up the
only draft of the first half of the manuscript of *Of Mice
And Men*. Steinbeck wrote, "Two months of work to do
over again. I was pretty mad at the time but the poor fellow may have been acting critically." Steinbeck rewrote the
manuscript and turned it in to his publishing house, and
the book was subsequently published. When the early re-
views were tepid in their praise. Steinbeck observed, "I'm
not sure Toby didn't know what he was doing when he ate
the first draft."
    Quoted in *The Writer's Home Companion*,
    by Jᴀᴍᴇs Cʜᴀʀʟᴛᴏɴ & Lɪʙʙʏ Mᴀʀᴋ

When director Tom Carlson discovered that his dog had
chewed up a prized autographed copy of one of Ogden
Nash's books, he discovered that the book was out of print.
He tracked down a replacement and mailed it off to Nash,
asking him to autograph it. He explained in a letter what
his dog had done to his first copy. Nash returned the book

with the inscription, "To Tom Carlson, or his dog – depending on whose taste it best suits."

At this point our so-called good girl was dipping into a copy of Nora Roberts's *Midnight Bayou*. Very studious. She'd torn off the cover and was working her way through chapter 2. Rarely have I see someone so thoroughly enjoy a book.

    MARTIN KIHN, *Bad Dog (A Love Story)*

Though he had very little Latin beyond "Cave canem," he had, as a young dog, devoured Shakespeare (in a tasty leather binding).

    DODIE SMITH, *The Hundred and One Dalmatians*

To Rufus, who edited Chapter 27.

    JEFFREY KONVITZ, in the dedication to his Great
    Pyrenees in his novel *The Guardian*. Rufus chewed the
    chapter to pieces and Konvitz needed to rewrite it from
    scratch. He claimed it was better
    "the second time around."

Dogs & Cats

A good recipe for a human reducing breakfast is a lot of good things to eat, and three spaniels and two cats to eat with.
  GLADYS TABER, *The Book of Stillmeadow*

Dogs eat. Cats dine.
  ANN TAYLOR

It's like I said all along, poopsie: cats rule and dogs drool.
  SASSY TO CHANCE, *Homeward Bound*

Let us love dogs; let us love only dogs! Men and cats are unworthy creatures.
  MARIE BASHKIRTSEFF, in Mary Serrano's
  The Journal of a Young Artist

I love both the way a dog looks up at me and a cat condescends to me.

GLADYS TABER, *The Book of Stillmeadow*

Dogs will come when called. Cats will take a message and get back to you.

MISSY DIZICK and MARY BLY,
Dogs Are Better Than Cats

Cats are smarter than dogs. You can't get eight cats to pull a sled through snow.

JEFF VALDEZ

Charley has no interest in cats, whatever, even for chasing purposes.

JOHN STEINBECK, on his poodle Charley

[I am a] dog man, and all felines can tell this at a glance—a sharp, vindictive glance.

JAMES THURBER

You know, it was raining cats and dogs the other day. I know because I stepped in a poodle.

STEVE MARTIN, told to an audience of dogs

Every dog must have his day.

JONATHAN SWIFT

Dog will have his day.

WILLIAM SHAKESPEARE.

Every dog has his day – but the nights are reserved for the cats.

UNKNOWN

Man loves the dog because the dog is foolish enough to trust Man. On the other hand, the cat obeys the Scriptures: "Put not they trust in things." The cat is like the wise man: he trusts a principle; not a man of principle.

MELVIN B. TOLSON, *Tigers and Lions and Men*

Cats seem to go on the principle that it never does any harm to ask for what you want.

JOSEPH WOOD KRUTCH, American naturalist author

It often happens that a man is more humanely related to a cat or dog than to any human being.

HENRY DAVID THOREAU

It's funny how dogs and cats know the inside of folks better than other folks do.

ELEANOR H. PORTER, *Pollyanna*

Women and cats will do as they please, and men and dogs should relax and get used to the idea.

ROBERT A. HEINLEIN

Everyone should have a dog that will worship him and a cat that will ignore him.

DEREKE BRUCE, on keeping one's importance in perspective

Cat's motto: No matter what you've done wrong, always try and make it look like the dog did it.

ANONYMOUS

I care not for a man's religion whose dog and cat are not the better for it.

ABRAHAM LINCOLN

Prose books are the show dogs I breed and sell to support my cat.

ROBERT GRAVES, on his love for poetry

The cat is the mirror of his human's mind . . .the dog mirrors his human appearance.

WINIFRED CARRIERE

The dog is mentioned in the bible eighteen times – the cat not even once.

W.E. FARBSTEIN

Dogs & Women

I am I because my little dog knows me.
GERTRUDE STEIN

A dog, I will maintain, is a very tolerable judge of beauty, as appears from the fact that any liberally educated dog does, in a general way, prefer a woman to a man.
FRANCES THOMPSON, *New York Times Magazine,* May 14, 1967

Love is the emotion a woman feels for a poodle dog and sometimes for a man.
GEORGE JEAN NATHAN

The woman who is really kind to dogs is always one who has failed to inspire sympathy in men.
MAX BEERBOHM

She did not observe Mr. Farebrother's approach along the grass, and just stooped down to lecture a small black-and-tan terrier, which would persist in walking on the sheet and smelling at the rose leaves as Mary sprinkled them. She took his forepaws in one hand, and lifted the forefinger of the other, while the dog wrinkled his brows and look embarrassed. "Fly, Fly, I am ashamed of you," Mary was saying in a grave contralto. "This is not becoming in a sensible dog; anybody would think you were a silly young gentleman." "You are unmerciful to young gentlemen, Miss Garth" said the Vicar within two yards of her. Mary started up and blushed. "It always answers to reason with Fly," she said laughingly.

    GEORGE ELIOT, *Middlemarch*

And I am simply delighted that you have a Springer spaniel. That is the perfect final touch to our friendship. Do you know there is always a barrier between me and any man or woman who does not like dogs.

    ELLEN GLASGOW

I once decided not to date a guy because he wasn't excited to meet my dog. I mean, this was like not wanting to meet my mother.

    BONNIE SCHACTER, Founder of the Single Pet
    Owner's Society Singles Group

I've been on so many blind dates, I should get a free dog.

    WENDY LIEBMAN

There are no one-night stands with a dog. Once you let your pet into your bed, it is hard to get him out.

DIANA DELMAR, *The Guilt-Free Dog Owner's Guide*

You enter into a certain amount of madness when you marry a person with pets.

NORA EPHRON

All men are not slimy warthogs. Some men are silly giraffes, some woebegone puppies, some insecure frogs. But if one is not careful, those slimy warthogs can ruin it for all the others.

CYNTHIA HEIMEL, *Get Your Tongue Out Of My Mouth, I'm Kissing You Goodbye!*

Diamonds are a girl's best friend. Dogs are a man's best friend. Now you know which sex is smarter.

NANCY GREY, *Stupid Men Jokes*

I never married because there was no need. I have three pets at home that answer the same purpose as a husband. I have a dog that growls every morning, a parrot that swears all afternoon, and a cat that comes home late at night.

MARIE CORELLI

Ah, wonderful women! Just give me a comfortable couch, a dog, a good book, and a woman. Then if you can get the dog to go somewhere and read the book, I might have a little fun!

GROUCHO MARX

PAUL SCARRON, a celebrated 17th century French poet, once published a collection of his work and dedicated it to his sister's dog. The dedication read "For my sister's bitch." While the book was in production, Scarron and his sister had a falling out. The publisher could not change the dedication, but agreed to insert an errata slip with a new dedication in the book It read, "My bitch of a sister."

But chicks know that guys are like dogs. You know, you take a dog, you beat the shit out him – Pow! Pow! – but he'll keep coming back. Ladies are like cats. You yell at a cat once – Siamese cat – phsst! They're gone.

LENNY BRUCE, *The Essential Lenny Bruce*

Smart Dogs

Many of my clients are skeptical when I tell them that dogs live only in the present and that their real memory span is very short—about 20 seconds. After all, they argue, my dog is trained to retrieve a ball and drop it at my feet every time I throw it. They do remember what to do. But that is not what is happening in their brains.

CESAR MILLAN, *Short Guide to a Happy Dog*

'Look, Mr. Edison,' said Sparky. 'Why not keep quiet about this? It's been working out to everybody's satisfaction for hundreds of thousands of years. Let sleeping dogs lie. You forget all about it, destroy the intelligence analyzer, and I'll tell you what to use for a lamp filament.'

KURT VONNEGUT, "Tom Edison's Shaggy Dog," *Kurt Vonnegut: Novels and Stories, 1963-1973*. Edison had just discovered that dogs are smarter than humans.

I've seen a look in dogs' eyes, a quickly vanishing look of amazed contempt, and I am convinced that basically dogs think humans are nuts.

JOHN STEINBECK

We always fancied Marley to be dumb as algae, but he had been clever enough to figure out how to use his long, strong tongue through the bars to slowly work the barrels free from their slots. He had licked his way to freedom.

JOHN GROGAN, *Marley and Me*

I like to joke about my dog's IQ as much as the next person – she doesn't take it personally. But believing your dog is an imbecile does spoil the party a little bit.

JOHN HOMANS, *What's a Dog For?*

It is probably true, then, that dogs don't think about art, the origin of the universe, or geopolitics.

ROGER CARAS, *A Dog Is Listening*

There have always been considerable differences of opinion as to whether a dog really thinks. I, personally, have no doubt that distinct mental processes do go on inside the dog's brain, although many times these processes are hardly worthy of the name. I have known dogs, especially puppies, who were almost as stupid as humans in their mental reactions.

ROBERT BENCHLEY, *Your Boy and His Dog*

They say a reasonable amount of fleas is good for a dog – keeps him from broodin' over being a dog, mebbe.

EDWARD NOYES WESTCOTT, American novelist

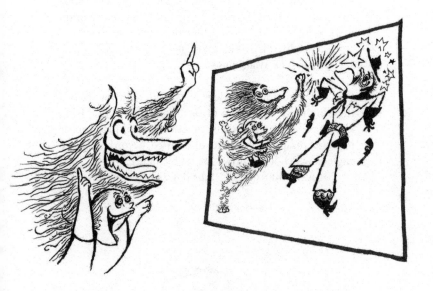

I too could've gone to school and become educated. I could've studied *The Odyssey,* and *Lord Jim,* and *Bleak House.* But just because I'm a dog, they say I can't go to their stupid school. On the other hand, when they need a shortstop, then they don't seem to mind so much that I'm a dog. In fact, sometimes being a dog can be a distinct advantage.

SNOOPY, *Snoopy: the Musical*

I'll tell you what – how would it be to issue special collars to all dogs who have graduated from my college? Something distinctive which everybody would recognize. See what I mean? Sort of a badge of honor. Fellow with a dog entitled to wear the Ukridge collar would be in a position to look down on the bloke whose dog hadn't got one.

P.G. WODEHOUSE, "Ukridge's Dog College,"
The Best Of Wodehouse

One of the reasons that dogs are given credit for serious thinking is the formation of their eyebrows. A dog lying in front of a fire and looking up at his master may appear pathetic, disapproving, sage, or amused, according to the angle at which its eyebrows are set by nature.

ROBERT BENCHLEY, *Your Boy and His Dog*

Love & Loyalty

It is a strange thing, love. Nothing but love has made the dog lose his wild freedom, to become the servant of man. And his very servility or completeness of love makes a term of deepest contempt – "You dog!"
 D.H. LAWRENCE, *The Greatest Dog Stories Ever Told*

To a man the greatest blessing is individual liberty, to a dog it is the last word in despair.
 WILLIAM LYON PHELPS, *Of Cats and Men*, compiled by Frances E Clarke

Dogs are the most amazing creatures; they give uncondi-
tional love. For me they are the role model for being alive.

GILDA RADNER, *It's Always Something*

Animals are such agreeable friends; they ask no questions,
pass no criticisms.

GEORGE ELIOT

You can read every day where a dog saved the life of a
drowning child, or lay down his life for his master. Some
people call this loyalty. I don't. I may be wrong, but I call it
love – the deepest kind of love.

WILSON RAWLS, *Where the Red Fern Grows*

Excavators digging through the volcanic ash that buried
the ruins of Pompeii in A.D. 79 discovered a dog lying
across a child. The dog, whose name was Delta, wore a collar that told how he had saved the life of his owner, Severi-
nus, three times.

JOHN RICHARD STEPHENS, author and editor

Histories are more full of examples of the fidelity of dogs
than of friends.

ALEXANDER POPE, in a letter to H. Cromwell, 1709

To be sure, the dog is loyal. But why, on that account,
should we take him as an example? He is loyal to men, not
to other dogs.

KARL KRAUS

When I hear tell of the character and devotion of dogs, I remain unmoved. All of my dogs have been scamps and thieves and troublemakers and I've adored them all.

HELEN HAYES, *On Reflection*

Thorns may hurt you, men desert you, sunlight turn to fog; but you're never friendless ever, if you have a dog.

DOUGLAS MALLOCH, *In Forest Land (1906)*

Scratch a dog and you'll find a permanent job.

FRANKLIN P. JONES

Verily there are rewards for our doing good to animals, and giving them water to drink. An adulteress was forgiven who passed by a dog at a well; for the dog was holding out his tongue from thirst, which was nearly killing him; and the woman took off her boot and tied it to the end of her garment and drew water for the dog, and gave him to drink; and she was forgiven because of that act.

The Sunna (or Holy Traditions of Mohammed)

Many dogs are used as decorations but by far the greatest number are a sop for loneliness. A man's or woman's confidant. An audience for the shy. A child to the childless.

JOHN STEINBECK,
Random Thoughts on Random Dogs

It isn't orthodox to ascribe a soul to a dog. But Hub was loving and loyal, with a jealousy that tests it quality. He was reverent, patient, faithful. He was sympathetic, more than humanly so sometimes, for no lure could be devised to call him from the sick bed of mistress or master. He minded his own affairs – especially worthy of human emulation.

WARREN G. HARDING, writing after the death of his dog Hub, who was poisoned.

Dogs are indeed the most social, affectionate and amiable animals of the whole brute creation...

EDMUND BURKE

The one absolutely unselfish friend that man can have in this selfish world, the one that never deserts him, the one that never proves ungrateful or treacherous is his dog. A man's dog stands by him in prosperity and in poverty, in health and in sickness. When all other friends desert, he remains. When riches take wings, and reputation falls to pieces, he is as constant in his love as the sun in its journey through the heavens.

GEORGE GRAHAM VEST, 19th century Missouri congressman in a famous closing argument in a case where a dog owner sued a man who killed his dog.

A devoted dog. One that will sit in front of you all evening while you are trying to read, looking at you with anxious, supplicating eyes until you feel like a brute for ignoring him. Did someone say that bestowing a few pats and affectionate words will reassure your loyal friend and enable you to go on reading? Only a dedicated and mindless propagandist for man's most insatiable dependent – and the country is full of just such propagandists – would venture such a preposterous claim.

    CHARLTON OGBURN, Jr.,
    American journalist and author

They motivate us to play, be affectionate, seek adventure and be loyal.

    TOM HAYDEN

He has every characteristic of a dog except loyalty.

    HENRY FONDA, in *The Best Man*

There is nothing more ill-bred than trying to steal the affections of one's dog.

    HUGH BONNEVILLE, (Robert, Earl of Graham)
    in *Downton Abbey*

There is no faith which has never yet been broken, except that of a truly faithful dog.

    KONRAD LORENZ

Dogs have given us their absolute all. We are the center of their universe, we are the focus of their love and faith and trust. They serve us in return for scraps. It is without a doubt the best deal man has ever made.

ROGER CARAS, *A Celebration of Dogs*

He had a terrible, terrible necessity to love, and this trammelled the native, savage hunting beast which he was. He was torn between two great impulses: the native impulse to hunt and kill, and the strange, secondary supervening impulse to love and obey.

D.H. LAWRENCE, *The Greatest Dog Stories Ever Told*

Personal friendship means everything to a dog; but remember, it entails no small responsibility, for a dog is not a servant to whom you can easily give notice. And remember, too, if you are an over- sensitive person, that the life of your friend is much shorter than your own and a sad parting, after ten or fifteen years, is inevitable.

KONRAD LORENZ, *King Solomon's Ring*

If my dogs have been faithful to me, I'd been faithful to them. We'd all kept our promises and then some. I felt good about that.

JON KATZ, *A Dog Year*

Talking with Dogs

It has been decided that since the talking pictures have come into their own, particularly with this organization, that the making of animal pictures, such as we have in the past with Rin Tin Tin, is not in keeping with the policy that has been adopted for us for talking pictures, very obviously, of course, because dogs don't talk.

P.A. CHASE, a Warner Brothers executive, 1929

It is by muteness that a dog becomes for one so utterly beyond value; with him one is at peace, where words play no torturing tricks... Those are the moments that I think are precious to a dog – when, with his adoring soul comes through his eyes, he feels that you are really thinking of him.

JOHN GALSWORTHY, *Memories*

I used to look at [my dog] Smokey and think, 'If you were a little smarter you could tell me what you were thinking,' and he'd look at me like he was saying, 'If you were a little smarter, I wouldn't have to.'
FRED JUNGCLAUS

We expect our dogs to listen to us when we speak to them and our dogs, no less than we, do expect us to listen to them.
ROGER CARAS, *A Dog Is Listening*

I endeavor to fill in the thought bubble over her head as well as I can. Sometimes the message is fairly clear: want chicken. If she wants a run, she stands in front of me, ears slightly cocked, and fixes me with a hard stare, not angry but very definitive. If the delay is too long – sometimes an hour, sometimes five minutes – she unfurls an ululating whine, all o's and u's – the meaning of which is unmistakable. Why won't you take me?
JOHN HOMANS, *What's a Dog For?*

If dogs talked, one of them would be president by now.
DEAN KOONTZ

If dogs could talk, perhaps we would find it just as hard to get along with them as we do with people.
KAREL CAPEK, *Intimate Things*

If animals could speak, the dog would be a blundering outspoken fellow.
MARK TWAIN

If dogs could talk it would take a lot of the fun out of owning one.

ANDY ROONEY

The dog is a Yes-animal, very popular with people who can't afford a Yes-man.

ROBERTSON DAVIES,
The Table Talk of Samuel Marchbanks

He is so shaggy. People are amazed when he gets up and they suddenly realize they have been talking to the wrong end.

ELIZABETH JONES

My master made me this collar. He is a good and smart master and he made me this collar so that I may talk – SQUIRREL! . . . . False alarm.

DUG THE DOG, in the movie *Up*

[Dogs] never talk about themselves but listen to you while you talk about yourself, and keep up an appearance of being interested in the conversation.

JEROME K. JEROME

No one appreciates the very special genius of your conversation as the dog does.

CHRISTOPHER MORLEY, *Morley's Variety*

You can say any fool thing to a dog, and the dog will give you this look that says, `My God, you're RIGHT! I NEVER would've thought of that!'

DAVE BARRY

Dogs who cock their heads are engaged in a fierce inner struggle – not merely to comprehend, but to also remain calm and respectful. Were it not for the act of tilting their mugs in mock concentration (usually biting their tongues or the inside of their cheeks as well), they would run the potentially embarrassing risk of laughter – loud, long un-controllably – at nearly everything we say to them.

DANNY SHANAHAN, *Dogs We Love*

He smiled so big that it made him sneeze. It was like he was saying, "I know I'm a mess. Isn't it funny?" It's hard not to immediately fall in love with a dog who has a good sense of humor.

KATE DICAMILLO, *Because of Winn-Dixie*

A dog will smile. Romp with your dog a while and he or she will beam. Light up. You tell me the expression on that dog's face is not a smile. A mule or a monkey or a por-poise will sort of grin, but a dog is the only animal that will smile.

ROY BLOUNT, Jr., *Now, Where Were We?*

I am joy in a wooly coat, come to dance into your life, to make you laugh.

JULIE ADAMS CHURCH, *Uncommon Friends*

The dog has got more fun out of Man than Man has got out of the dog, for the clearly demonstrable reason that Man is the more laughable of the two animals.

JAMES THURBER, in his Introduction to
The Fireside Book of Dog Stories

One reason I love dogs is because they are hilarious. Every time I'm sure that we share the same soul, I notice he is chewing on an old Band-Aid.
MERRILL MARKOE

Dogs laugh but they laugh with their tails.
MAX EASTMAN, *Enjoyment of Living*

Say something idiotic and nobody but a dog politely wags his tail.
VIRGINIA GRAHAM, *Life After Harry*

In times of joy, all of us wished we possessed a tail we could wag.
W.H. AUDEN, *A Certain World*

'I wish we had tails to wag,' said Mr. Dearly.
  DODIE SMITH, *The Hundred and One Dalmatians*

Some dogs use their tails to let us know what's on their
minds Some wave their bulky bodies around and whip
themselves into an elaborate dance: "I want to go out!" "I
want something to eat!" Pet me, scratch me, rub my ears
now!" Dogs go in for exclamation points.
  ARTHUR YORINKS, *Dogs We Love*

Their tails are high and tongues awag – the twin banners
of sled dog contentment. Clara Germani, on Alaskan Huskies during the Iditarod race in Alaska Man himself cannot express love and humility by external signs so plainly
as does a dog, when with drooping ears, hanging lips, flex-
uous body, and wagging tail, he meets his beloved master.
Nor can these movements in the dog be explained by the
acts of volition or necessary instincts, any more than the
beaming eyes and smiling cheeks of a man when he meets
an old friend.
  CHARLES DARWIN, "The Expression of Emotions
  in Man and Animals," *Life and Letters of Charles
  Darwin*, Francis Darwin

Humans were denied the speech of animals. The only
common ground of communication upon which dog and
men can get together is in fiction.
  O. HENRY, *Memoirs of a Yellow Dog*

The argument was very sound,
And coming from a master's mouth
Would have been lauded for its truth.
But since the author was a hound,
Its merits went unrecognized.
> JEAN DE LA FONTAINE,
> *The Farmer, The Dog, and The Fox*

For company I have my dogs. For words, my books.
> ROBERT COANE

He is the one 'person' to whom I can talk without the conversation coming back to war.
> DWIGHT D. EISENHOWER, on his Scottie dog.

People can be a fine substitute for other dogs. But I think that if they had to choose, dogs by and large would choose the company of other dogs.
> ELIZABETH MARSHALL THOMAS,
> *The Hidden Life of Dogs*

An animal's eyes have the power to speak a great language.
> MARTIN BUBER

There are some dogs which, when you meet them, remind you that, despite thousands of years of manmade evolution, every dog is still only two meals away from being a wolf. These dogs advance deliberately, purposefully, the wilderness made flesh, their teeth yellow, their breath astink, while in the distance their owners witter, "He's an old soppy really, just poke him if he's a nuisance," and in the green of their eyes the red campfires of the Pleistocene gleam and flicker...

TERRY PRATCHETT & NEIL GAIMAN,
*Good Omens: The Nice and Accurate Prophesies of
Agnes Nutter, Witch*

He seemed neither old nor young. His strength lay in his eyes. They looked as old as the hills, and as young and as wild. I never tired of looking into them.

ALBERT PAYSON TERHUNE,
An Adventure With a Dog

I am secretly afraid of animals – of all animals except dogs and even some dogs. I think it is because of the us-ness in their eyes, with the underlying not-us-ness which belies it, and is so tragic a reminder of the lost age when we human beings branched off and left them: left them to eternal in-articulateness and slavery. "Why?" their eyes seem to ask us.

EDITH WHARTON

Travel with Dogs

Dogs love to go for rides. A dog will happily get into any vehicle going anywhere.

DAVE BARRY

Number one way that life would be different if dogs ran the world: All motorists must drive with head out window.

DAVID LETTERMAN

Mutt enjoyed traveling by car, but he was an unquiet passenger. He suffered from the delusion, common to dogs and small boys, that when he was looking out the right-hand side, he was probably missing something far more interesting on the left-hand side.

FARLEY MOWAT, *The Dog Who Wouldn't Be*

Dogs who chase cars see them as large, unruly ungulates badly in need of discipline and shepherding.

ELIZABETH MARSHALL THOMAS,
The Hidden Life of Dogs

DOROTHY PARKER had a Scottie named Alexander Woollcott Parker, named after her friend Alexander Woollcott. Woollcott said of the dog, 'He reversed the customary behavior of a namesake by christening me – three times, as I recall – in a single automobile ride.'

Did you ever notice when you blow in a dog's face he gets mad at you? But when you take him in a car he sticks his head out the window!

STEPHEN BLUESTONE, *The Flagrant Dead*

My Scottie refused to go for a walk with a friend of the house, but she would joyously accompany any stranger who drove a car.

MAZO DE LA ROCHE, Canadian novelist

Dogs feel very strongly that they should always go with you in the car, in case the need should arise for them to bark violently at nothing right in your ear.

DAVE BARRY

I won't leave Sweden without Ted. The dog is the closest thing in the world to me.

> LARS KARLSTRAND, who turned down a lucrative
> contract to play for a Scottish soccer team due
> to the six month quarantine laws in the UK.

Montmorency (the dog) came and sat on things just when they were wanted to be packed. He put his leg into the jam, and he worried the teaspoons, and he pretended that the lemons were rats, and got into the hamper and killed three of them.

> JEROME K. JEROME, *Three Men in a Boat*

I was faced with a grave moral problem as I did not know whether a dog bearing such a heavy coat as he had grown living in the snow could be brought to Cuba without making him suffer. But Blackie solved this problem when he saw us start packing by getting into the car and refusing to leave it unless he was lifted out. Lifted out, he would immediately leap back into the car and look at you with those eyes which are possessed only by springer spaniels and certain women.

> ERNEST HEMINGWAY, "The Christmas Gift"

There are only two rules. One is from E. M. Forster's guide to Alexandria; the best way to know Alexandria is to wander aimlessly. The second is from the Psalms; grin like a dog and run about through the city.

> JAN MORRIS, English travel writer

When I started driving our old four-door green DeSoto, I always took Skip on my trips around town. I would get Skip to prop himself against the steering wheel, his black head peering out of the windshield, while I crouched out of sight under the dashboard. Slowing the car to ten or fifteen, I would guide the steering wheel with my right hand while Skip, with his paws, kept it steady. As we drove by the Blue Front Café, I could hear one of the men shout: "Look at that ol' dog drivin' a car!"

WILLIE MORRIS, *My Dog Skip*

Man's Best Friend

The dog is man's best friend. This alone is depressing.

ANONYMOUS

The cat could very well be man's best friend but would never stoop to admitting it.

DOUG LARSON

When a man's best friend is his dog, that dog has a problem.

EDWARD ABBEY, *The Journey Home*

Outside of a dog, a book is a man's best friend. Inside of a dog, it's too dark to read.

GROUCHO MARX

The dog is man's best friend. He has a tail on one end.
Up in front he has teeth. And four legs underneath.

OGDEN NASH, "An Introduction to Dogs"

Dog may be Man's best friend, but Man is often Dog's severest critic, in spite of his historic protestations of affection and admiration. He calls an unattractive girl a dog, he talks acidly of dogs in the manger, he describes a hard way of life as a dog's life, he observes, cloudily, that this or that misfortune shouldn't happen to a dog, as if most slings and arrows should, and he describes anyone he can't stand as a dirty dog.

JAMES THURBER, *Thurber's Dogs*

A dog who thinks he is man's best friend is a dog who has obviously never met a tax lawyer.

FRAN LEBOWITZ, *Social Studies*

When a dog runs at you, whistle for him.

HENRY DAVID THOREAU

Dogs love company. They place it first in their short list of needs.

J.R. ACKERLEY, *My Dog Tulip*

Dogs, bless them, operate on the premise that human beings are fragile and require incessant applications of affection and reassurance. The random lick of the hand and the
furry chin draped over the instep are calculated to let the
shaky owner know that a friend is nearby.
  MARY MCGRORY, American journalist

I, who had my heart full for hours, took advantage of an
early moment of solitude, to cry in it very bitterly. Suddenly a little hairy head thrust itself from behind my pil-
lows into my face, rubbing its ears and nose against me
in responsive agitation, and drying the tears as they came.
  ELIZABETH BARRETT BROWNING

All his life he tried to be a good person. Many times, however, he failed. For after all, he was only human. He wasn't
a dog.
  CHARLES M. SCHULZ

I've always felt almost human. I've always known there's
something about me that's different than other dogs. Sure,
I'm stuffed into a dog's body, but that's just the shell. It's
what's inside that's important. The soul. And my soul is
very human.
  GARTH STEIN, *The Art of Racing in the Rain*

A dog is not 'almost human' and I know of no greater in-
sult to the canine race than to describe it as such.
  JOHN HOLMES, *Looking After Your Dog*

Jennie was a small Scottish terrier. Her jaw was skimpy, her haunches frail, her forelegs slightly bowed. She thought dimly and her coordination was only fair. Even in repose she had the strained, uncomfortable appearance of a woman on a bicycle.

JAMES THURBER,
The Dog that Wouldn't Come Home

In the world which we know, among the different and primitive geniuses that preside over the evolution of the several species, there exists not one, excepting that of the dog, that ever gave a thought to the presence of man.

MAURICE MAETERLINCK, *Our Friend, The Dog*

Fido and Rover are partaking of a mystery of which, further up the table, Cezanne and Beethoven are participants also.

REBECCA WEST, *The Strange Necessity*

Take our dogs and ourselves, connected as we are by a tie more intimate than most ties in this world, and yet, outside of that tie of friendly fondness, how insensible, each of us, to all that makes life significant for the other! – we to the rapture of bones under hedges, of smells of trees and lampposts, they to the delights of literature and art.

WILLIAM JAMES, "On a Certain Blindness in Human Beings"

Not Sure About Dogs

Anybody who hates children and dogs can't be all bad.
W.C. FIELDS, *W.C. Fields By Himself*

I never meant to say anything about this, but the fact is that I have never met a dog that didn't have it in for me.
JEAN KERR, *Please Don't Eat the Daisies*

It's the one species I wouldn't mind seeing vanish from the face of the earth. I wish they were like the White Rhino – six of them left in the Serengeti National Park, and all males.
ALAN BENNETT, on his antipathy towards dogs

I participate in all your hostility to dogs and would readily join in any plan of exterminating the whole race. I consider them the most afflicting of all follies for which men tax themselves.

>   THOMAS JEFFERSON, responding to a friend who
>   wrote to him complaining about stray dogs.

That indefatigable and unsavory engine of pollution, the dog.

>   JOHN SPARROW, in a letter to the *London Times*, 1975

Barking & Biting

All trees have bark.
All dogs bark.
Therefore, all dogs are trees.
The fallacy of barking up the wrong tree.
UNKNOWN

I never barked when out of season,
I never bit without a reason;
I ne'er insulted weaker brother,
nor wronged by force or fraud another. We brutes are
placed a rank below; Happy for man could he say so.
Robert Burns, from his poem On a Dog of Lord Eglinton's
No matter how eloquently a dog may bark, he cannot tell
you that his parents were poor, but honest.
BERTRAND RUSSELL

Many dogs can understand almost every word humans
say, while humans seldom learn to recognize more than a
half dozen barks, if that.
DODIE SMITH, *The Hundred and One Dalmatians*

It is a more remarkable fact that the dog, since being domesticated, has learned to bark in four or five distinct tones. With the domesticated dog we have the bark of eagerness, as in the chase; that of anger; the yelping or howling bark of despair, as when shut up; that of joy, as when starting on a walk with his master; and the very distinct one of demand or supplication, as when wishing for a door or window to be opened.

CHARLES DARWIN, *The Descent of Man*

Then, in a lull snatched for food, and still endeavoring to preserve some aspect of assurance, we heard the bark which meant: "Here is a door I cannot open!" We hurried forth and there he was on the top doorstep – busy, unashamed, giving no explanations, asking for his supper; and very shortly after him came his five hundred "Lost Dog" bills.

JOHN GALSWORTHY, *Memories*

And the fence allowed Millie to become "frenemies" with a fox. Millie knew where the invisible fence was buried under our lawn. And so, it seemed, did the fox. In the morning the two of them would stand twenty feet apart and bark happily at each other without danger of this turning into an unseemly brawl.

    P.J. O'ROURKE

Most dogs bark pointlessly, even if someone is walking by in the distance; but some, perhaps not the best watch dogs, yet rational creatures, quietly walk up to a stranger, sniff at him, and bark only if they smell something suspicious.

    FRANZ KAFKA, *The Diaries of Franz Kafka*

There's no sense in doing a lot of barking if you don't really have anything to say.

    SNOOPY

I'm a lean dog, a keen dog, a wild dog and alone;
I'm a rough dog, a tough dog hunting on my own;
I'm a bad dog, a mad dog, teasing silly sheep;
I love to sit and bay at the moon, to keep fat souls from sleep.

    IRENE McLEOD, "Lone Dog"
    Songs to Save a Soul (1915)

A barking dog is often more useful than a sleeping lion.

    WASHINGTON IRVING

'Tis sweet to hear the watch dog's honest bark
Bay deep-mouthed welcome as we draw near home; 'Tis
sweet to know there is an eye will mark
Our coming, and look brighter when we come.
    LORD BYRON

The dog barks backward without getting up
I can remember when he was a pup.
    ROBERT FROST

You will never reach your destination if you stop and
throw stones at every dog that barks.
    WINSTON CHURCHILL

The slowest barker is the surest biter.
    UNKNOWN

The dog, to gain some private ends,
Went mad and bit the man.
The man recovered of the bite,
The dog it was that died.
        OLIVER GOLDSMITH,
        An Elegy on the Death of a Mad Dog

They had a dog called Bluey. A known psychopath, Bluey
would attack himself if nothing else was available. He used
to chase himself in circles trying to bite his own balls off.
    CLIVE JAMES, *Unreliable Memoirs*

Charley is a born diplomat. He prefers negotiating to fighting, and properly so, since he is very bad at fighting. Only once in his ten years has he been in trouble – when he met a dog who refused to negotiate. Charley lost a piece of his right ear that time.

JOHN STEINBECK, *Travels With Charley*

We used to have a dog named Snoopy, you know, a real live dog. I suppose people who love Snoopy won't like it, but we gave him away. He fought with other dogs, so we traded him in for a load of gravel.

CHARLES M. SCHULZ

A dog is a dog except when he is facing you. Then he is Mr. Dog.

HAITIAN SAYING

A huge dog, tied by a chain was painted on the wall and over it was written in capital letters "Beware of the dog."

PETRONIUS ARBITER, first century

Breed not a savage dog, nor permit a loose stairway.

THE TALMUD

I loathe people who keep dogs. They are cowards who haven't got the guts to bite people themselves.

AUGUST STRINDBERG, *Inferno*

When a dog bites a man that is not news, but when a man bites a dog that is news.

> CHARLES DANA, 'What is News?', *The New York Sun*
> 1882 [also attributed to John Bogart,
> *New York Sun* city editor]

The man who gets bit twice by the same dog is better adapted for that kind of business than any other.

> JOSH BILLINGS, *Josh Billings' Sayings*

Like many Westies, he was woefully stubborn and never once came when called. He could be unpredictable and grouchy around small children and once bit my goddaughter's upper lip. He wasn't great with old people either; years later he bit an elderly woman, who, for some unexplicable reason, was standing bare-foot in her nightgown in our elevator when the door opened on our floor.

> JILL ABRAMSON, *The Puppy Diaries*

It made her so mad to see Muggs lying there, oblivious to the mice – they came running up to her – that she slapped him and he slashed at her, but didn't make it. He was sorry immediately, Mother said. He was always sorry, she said, after he bit someone, but we could not understand how she figured this out. He didn't act sorry.

> JAMES THURBER, *Thurber's Dogs*

If you pick up a starving dog and make him prosperous, he will not bite you; that is the principal difference between a dog and a man.

> MARK TWAIN, *Pudd'nhead Wilson*

Sit. Stay

Every human child must learn the universe fresh. Every stockdog pup carries the universe within him. Humans have externalized their wisdom – stored it in museums, libraries, the expertise of the learned. Dog wisdom is inside the blood and bones.

DONALD McCAIG, *Eminent Dogs, Dangerous Men: Searching through Scotland for a Border Collie*

A dog teaches a boy fidelity, perseverance, and to turn around three times before lying down – very important traits in times like these. In fact, just as soon as a dog comes along who, in addition to these qualities, also knows when to buy and sell stocks, he can move right up to the boy's bedroom and the boy can sleep in the dog house.

ROBERT BENCHLEY, *Your Boy and His Dog.* Also used in his introduction to *Artemus Ward, His Book.*

First, you learn a new language, profanity: and second you learn not to discipline your dogs when you're mad, and that's most of the time when you are training dogs.

LOU SCHULTZ, trainer of Alaskan Huskies

In order to really enjoy a dog, one doesn't merely try to train him to be semi-human. The point is to open oneself to the possibility of becoming partly a dog.

TED HOAGLAND, *The Edward Hoagland Reader*

Place the puppy on newspaper every two hours. Soon he will perform as regularly as Old Faithful. When he has learned the purpose of of a newspaper, he may go out of his way to find one. At this time, caution must be exercised about leaving newspapers on living room sofas.

STEPHEN BAKER, *How to Live With a Neurotic Dog*

Dogs that we raise from puppyhood reflect our willingness to know and love and train them properly. Dogs we rescue or inherit are often more complex, and can challenge us even more.

Jon Katz, *The Dogs of Bedlam Farm*

To dogs, there are only two positions in a relationship: leader and follower. Dominant and submissive. There is no in-between in their world. When a dog lives with a human, in order for the human to be able to control the dog's behavior, she must make the commitment to take on the role of pack leader, 100 percent of the time. It's that simple.

Cesar Millan, *Cesar's Way*

Although dominant dogs do well in conventional dog-training schools, they do not generally bring their newfound manners home, and dominance-related problems usually persist. They will obey commands perhaps 70 percent of the time and only when they feel like it. When you really need them to do something, however, they just ignore you.

Dr. Nicholas Dodman,
The Dog Who Loved Too Much

In dog training, jerk is a noun, not a verb.

Dr. Dennis Fetko, author and animal behaviorist

Rambunctious, rumbustious, delinquent dogs become angelic when sitting.

Dr. Ian Dunbar, *After You Get Your Puppy*

There are times when even the best manager is like the little boy with the big dog. waiting to see where the dog wants to go so he can take him there.

LEE IACOCCA, auto executive and author

I had my copy of *Gun Dog* by Richard Wolters. I did every-thing the revered Wolters said. That meant (to my wife's horror) I had a ziplock bag of frozen grouse wings in the freezer. I attached one to a fishing pole line and stood in the yard swinging it in circles – the way Wolters claims gives a puppy its first chance to point. Millie pointed. But in the opposite direction of the spinning wing. And on the next rotation she ate it.

P.J. O'ROURKE

I do not believe in paying off a dog by shoving food into his mouth every time he does something he was bred to do. I like to think that the training is taking place in his head, not the stomach. A kind word in his ear is making the brain work; food in the stomach only makes the bow-els work.

RICHARD WOLTORS, *Gun Dog*

Owners who pet dogs indiscriminately are, unbeknownst to themselves, rewarding their dog for nothing. Dogs that are petted for nothing have much less incentive to work for a reward. People are like this, too.

Dr. NICHOLAS DODMAN,
The Dog Who Loved Too Much

Sit. Stay.

What else is obedience training but the attempt to bend the dog's will to our own? We tell them to "sit" and "stay" at our command. We demand that they "shake" by putting out a paw every time we ask – so it's not really asking, it's telling.

> Sue Halpern, *A Dog Walks into a Nursing Home*

A dog, more than any other creature, it seems to me, gets interested in one subject, theme, or object, in life, and pursues it with a fixity of purpose which would be inspiring to Man if it weren't so troublesome.

> E.B. White, *One Man's Meat*

Do not let your dog give you commands. Dogs will often try to get our attention by nudging us, putting their heads in our laps, or jumping up. When your dog does this, ignore her; do not even say, "no." Just don't acknowledge the behavior. Otherwise, your dog has just told you what to do, and you did it.

> Cesar Millan, *Short Guide to a Happy Dog*

When you point out something to a dog, he looks at your finger.

> J Bryan III, *Hodgepodge Two: Another Commonplace book*

Properly trained, a man can be a dog's best friend.

> Corey Ford, *The Corey Ford Sporting Treasury*

I don't give my dogs much training because I want them
to do their own thinking, to do what they want rather than
wait to see what I want. If I train them, they learn from me.
If I don't train them, I learn from them.
ELIZABETH MARSHALL THOMAS,
The Social Lives of Dogs

Dogs, like human infants, learn by imitation. Show him
what you want; whether or not he performs, he will be
duly amused by your hilarious attempts to please him.
STEPHEN BAKER, *How To Live With A Neurotic Dog*

Why, that dog is practically a Phi Beta Kappa. She can sit
up and beg, and she can give her paw – I don't say she will
but she can.
DOROTHY PARKER, "Toward The Dog Days,"
McCall's, July 1928

He came consistently on command (unless there was
something riveting his attention, such as another dog, cat,
squirrel, butterfly, mailman, or floating weed seed); he sat
consistently (unless he felt strongly like standing); and
heeled reliably (unless there was something so tempting
it was worth strangling himself over – see dogs, cats, squir-
rels, etc, above).
JOHN GROGAN, *Marley and Me*

If you grasp a crossbow and call a bird,
Or brandish a club and beckon a dog,
Then what you want to come will go away instead.
The Huainanzi: A Guide to the Theory and Practice

Sit. Stay.

of Government in Early Han China, by John S. Major,
Sarah A. Queen, Andrew Seth Meyer, and Harold D.
Roth, editors and translators. The Huainanzi is a
Chinese philosophical work, completed in 139 BC

Do not make the mistake of treating your dogs like humans or they will treat you like dogs.
MARTHA SCOTT, actress

I can train any dog in five minutes. It's training the owner
that takes longer.
BARBARA WOODHOUSE, *No Bad Dogs*

Someday, if I ever get the chance, I shall write a book, or
warning, on the character and temperament of the dachshund and why he can't be trained and shouldn't be. I would
rather train a striped zebra to balance an Indian club than
induce a dachshund to heed my slightest command.
E.B. WHITE, *E.B. White on Dogs,* by Martha White

I like to read books on dog training. Being the owner of
dachshunds, to me a book on dog discipline becomes a
volume of inspired humor. Every sentence is a riot.
E.B. WHITE, *E.B. White on Dogs,* by Martha White

If a human brain is plastic – able to change through learn-
ing – so must a dog's be. the common refrain that "you
can't teach an old dog new tricks" began to seem like
an excuse for human laziness. Why couldn't dogs learn
throughout their lives, like we could?
SUE HALPERN, *A Dog Walks into a Nursing Home*

No one ever called him a great dog – or even a good dog. He was as wild as a banshee and as strong as a bull. He crashed joyously through life with a gusto most often associated with natural disasters. He's the only dog I've ever known to get expelled from obedience school.

JOHN GROGAN, *Marley and Me*

An animal on a leash is not tamed by the owner. The owner is extending himself through the leash to that part of his personality which is pure dog, that part of him which just wants to eat, sleep, bark, hump chairs, wet the floor in joy, and drink out of a toilet bowl.

DIANE ACKERMAN, *A Natural History of Love*

A well-trained and well-treated sheep dog is more of a dog than a wild one, just as a stray, terrified by ill-usage, or a spoilt lap dog has had his "dogginess" debased.

W.H. AUDEN, *A Certain World*

A sheepdog can work for a man and not give a damn for him. Must the actor love the director?

DONALD MCCAIG, *Nop's Hope*

When training a dog, it is important to leave it wanting to do more. In other words, train your dog until it is tired; you want your dog to want to work, not to have to work.

JANET RUCKERT, *Are You My Dog?*

Sit. Stay.

Never repeat a command. Most dogs are not deaf; they just choose not to listen.

    CONNIE JANKOWSKI
    Treat Your Partner Like a Dog

The "problem" of caring for a dog has been unnecessarily complicated. Take the matter of housebreaking. In the suburbia of those lovely post-Victorian days of which I write the question of housebreaking a puppy was met with the simple bold courage characteristic of our forefathers. You simply kept the house away from the puppy. This was not only the simplest way, it was the only practical way.

    E.B. WHITE, "The Care and Training of a Dog"

When a doting person gets down on all fours and plays with the dog's rubber mouse, it only confuses the puppy and gives him a sense of insecurity. He gets the impression that the world is unstable and wonders whether he is supposed to walk on his hind legs and smoke cigars.

    COREY FORD, *The Corey Ford Sporting Treasury*

Most dog owners are at length able to teach themselves to obey their dog.

    ROBERT MORLEY

Any time you think you have influence, try ordering around someone else's dog.

    HARRY OTIS, *Simple Truths: The Best of the Cockle Bur*

I had a dog who was savage and averse to all strangers, and I purposely tried his memory after an absence of five years and two days. I went near the stable where he lived, and shouted to him in my old manner. He showed no joy, but instantly followed me out walking and obeyed me, as if I'd parted only a half hour before.

CHARLES DARWIN, "The Expression of Emotions in Man and Animals," *Life and Letters of Charles Darwin*, Francis Darwin

I cannot stress often enough that if you wish to keep a dog that is not normal, you must face up to living a slightly restricted existence. Although you may love a subnormal dog, other people must not be inconvenienced by it.

BARBARA WOODHOUSE, *No Bad Dogs*

Breeds

Any dog person will not only tell you that the various breeds differ greatly in their intelligence but will harangue you about the merits of some breeds and the limitations of others. Such people are using the word intelligence to mean trainability.

STANLEY COREN, *The Intelligence of Dogs*

All dogs are working dogs. Nearly every breed – even lap dogs – were developed for specific tasks. Every dog is descended from creatures who aided primitive, frightened humans when they most needed it. Today, when we are less primitive but still frightened, they are working harder than ever.

JON KATZ, *The New Work of Dogs*

My father was a St. Bernard, my mother was a collie, but I am a Presbyterian.

MARK TWAIN, "A Dog's Tale"

If you are a police dog, where's your badge?

JAMES THURBER, a regular question he asked his dog.

Among God's creatures two, the dog and the guitar, have taken all the sizes and all the shapes in order not to be separated from Man.

ANDRES SEGOVIA

One of the saddest sights is to see a Dane ill. Their big eyes are a picture of misery, for make no mistake, a sick Dane puts everything it can to get all the love and sympathy when it is ill.

BARBARA WOODHOUSE, *Talking to Animals*

Things that upset a terrier may pass virtually unnoticed by the Great Dane.

DR. SMILEY BLANTON, *Love or Perish*

The nose of the bulldog has been slanted backwards so that he can breathe without letting go.

WINSTON CHURCHILL

It is best to remember that even though an English Bulldog may remind us of Winston Churchill, it would not really make an effective Prime Minister.

DANIEL TORTORA, *The Right Dog For You*

I wonder if other dogs think poodles are members of a weird religious cult.
  RITA RUDNER

The pug is living proof that God has a sense of humor.
  MARGO KAUFMAN

Fox terriers are born with about four times as much original sin in them as other dogs.
  JEROME K. JEROME, *Three Men in a Boat*

They have all the compactness of a small dog and all the valor of a big one. And they are so exceedingly sturdy that it is proverbial that the only thing fatal to them is being run over by an automobile – in which the case the car itself knows that it has been in a fight.
  DOROTHY PARKER, on Scottish Terriers,
  "Toward The Dog Days," *McCall's*, July 1928

Dachshunds are ideal dogs for small children, as they are already stretched and pulled to such length that the child can't do much harm one way or the other. The dachshund being so long also makes difficult for a very small child to go through with the favorite juvenile maneuver of lifting the dog's hind legs up in the air and wheeling it along like a barrow, cooing, "Diddy-ap."

ROBERT BENCHLEY, *Your Boy and his Dog*

Dalmatians are not only superior to other dogs, they are like other dogs, infinitely less stupid than men.

EUGENE O'NEILL

Many people, I know, disparage Pekes, but take it from me. They are all right. If they have a fault, it is a tendency to think too much of themselves.

P.G. WODEHOUSE

A Pekingese is not a pet dog; it is an undersized lion.

A.A. MILNE

Even the tiniest poodle is lionhearted, ready to do anything to defend home, master, and mistress.

LOUIS SABIN, *All About Dogs As Pets*

Why not be oneself? That is the whole secret of a successful appearance. If one is a greyhound, why try and look like a Pekingese.

EDITH SITWELL

If you can't decide between a Shepherd, a Setter, or a Poodle, get them all. . . Adopt a mutt.

ASPCA

One is probably less likely to obtain in a mongrel a nervous, mentally deficient animal than in a dog with eight champions in its pedigree.

KONRAD LORENZ, *Man Meets Dog*

Most cross-bred dogs have a thing called hybrid vigor, which helps them fight disease.

JAMES HERRIOT, *Wes*

Yes, he's got all of them different kinds of thoroughbred blood in him, and he's got other kinds you ain't mentioned and that you ain't slick enough to see. You may think you're running him down, but what you say just proves he ain't a common dog.

DON MARQUIS, "Blood will Tell."

Those so-called mongrels, by the way, are prone to be cleverer and stronger than any thoroughbred. Rightly trained, they are ideal chums and pets and guards – a truth too little known.

ALBERT PAYSON TERHUNE, "The Fighting Strain."

I like a bit of mongrel myself, whether it's a man or a dog: they're the best for everyday.

GEORGE BERNARD SHAW, *Misalliance*

Two of my best friends are dogs of a whirling melange of ancestry. They are short in the paw, long and wavering in the body, heavy and worried in the head. They are willing, useless, and irresistible. Nobody ever asks their breed.

DOROTHY PARKER, in her introduction to
Thurber's *Men, Women and Dogs*

A man once told me that his dog was half pit bull and half Poodle. He claimed that it wasn't much good as a guard dog, but it was a vicious gossip.

STANLEY COREN, *How To Speak Dog*

I think that the great popularity enjoyed by some comical breeds of dogs is attributable to a large extent to our longing for gaiety.

KONRAD LORENZ, *Man Meets Dog*

The uglier the dog, the more he or she is loved.

MARTY LEWIS

Breeds

A dog is a smile and a wagging tail. What is in between doesn't matter much.

CLARA ORTEGA

To call him a dog hardly seems to do him justice, though inasmuch as he had four legs, a tail, and barked. I admit he was, to all outward appearances. But to those of us who knew him well, he was a perfect gentleman.

HERMIONE GINGOLD, *The World is Square*

A really companionable and indispensable dog is an accident of nature. You can't get it by breeding and you can't buy it with money. It just happens along.

E.B. WHITE, "The Care and Training of a Dog"

The idea is that people actively bred wolves to become dogs just the way they now breed dogs to be tiny or large, or to herd sheep. The prevailing scientific opinion now, however, is that this origin story does not pass muster. Wolves are hard to tame, even as puppies, and many researchers find it much more plausible that dogs, in effect, invented themselves.

JAMES GORMAN, *The New York Times*,
January 22, 2016

Those Who Work and Those Who Wait

My dogs are the only living creatures on the planet whose need to love and be loved comes as close to bottomless as my own. At the end of every day, I am greeted at the front door as if I am a long-lost friend who, mistakenly, was believed to have been dead for years. I sometimes want to tell my dogs that I am undeserving of this avalanche of affection, but I can't bring myself to break the bad news.

ALEC MAPA, "There's No Place Like Home, Judy"

Since dogs probably don't understand the concept of time – at least not in the way that human beings do – when I leave our house, Ella assumes I've left her forever. This is why she goes berserk with joy when I return home – whether I've been gone three weeks or three hours.

MICHAEL KONIK, *Ella in Europe*

What does a dog do on his day off? He can't lie around –
that's his job.

GEORGE CARLIN

He toils not, neither does he spin, yet Solomon in all his
glory never lay upon a door-mat all day long, sun-soaked
and fly-fed and fat, while his master worked for the means
wherewith to purchase an idle wag of Solomonic tail, sea-
soned with a look of tolerant recognition.

AMBROSE BIERCE

We could have bought a small yacht with what we spent
on our dog and all the things he destroyed. Then again,
how many yachts wait by the door all day for your return?

JOHN GROGAN, *Marley and Me*

Charley is a mind-reading dog. There have been many
trips in his lifetime, and often he has to be left at home. He
knows we are going long before the suitcase has come out,
and he paces and worries and whines and goes into a state
of mild hysteria.

JOHN STEINBECK, *Travels with Charley*

The great fear dogs know is. . . that you will not come back
when you go out the door without them.

STANLEY COREN, *The Intelligence of Dogs*

The dog lives for the day, the hour; even the moment.

ROBERT FALCON SCOTT

In all likelihood dogs do not make comparative assessments about their lives. . . do not lie around wishing they were somewhere else, fantasizing about better owners, dreaming of more varied settings.

CAROLINE KNAPP, *Pack of Two*

Dogs lead a nice life. You never see a dog with a wrist watch.

GEORGE CARLIN

Hey, Max!
Hey Gidget!
Any plans, today?
Yes. Big, big stuff today, Gidget. I've got big plans. I'm gonna to sit here and I'm gonna wait for Katie to come back.
Oh, that sounds exciting. Well, I won't interrupt. I've got a very big day, too

A conversation between Max, a dog, and Gidget, a cat, in *The Secret Life of Pets*

He had let out the dogs and they were jumping around him frantic with joy, as if they were afraid, every night, there would never be another letting out or another morning.

MARY O'HARA, *My Friend Flicka*

I wake up sometimes in the middle of the night and think about Parker. He was a good friend. I understand how you feel. Hachi, my friend, Parker is never coming home. But if Hachiko wants to wait, then Hachiko should wait. You want to wait for him, don't you? Have a long life, Hachi.

RICHARD GERE as Ken, in *Hachi: A Dog's Tale*

He was like the dog who would not leave the place where his master was buried. . .

JULES VERNE, *The Mysterious Island*

Did you ever walk into a room and forget why you walked in? I think that is how dogs spend their lives.

SUE MURPHY, writer and comedian

The devotion of a dog has been greatly exaggerated. What a dog really wants is excitement. He is easily bored, cannot amuse himself, and therefore demands entertainment. The dog's ideal is a life of active uselessness.

WILLIAM LYON PHELPS, *Of Cats and Men*, compiled by Frances E. Clarke

My first job was cleaning dog kennels. It was especially, ah, aromatic during those hot, humid Louisiana summers, but it prepared me for Hollywood.

ROBERT CRAIS, American mystery writer

About the only thing on a farm that has an easy time is the dog.

EDGAR HOWE, *The Story of a Country Town*

Everybody in my family paints, except perhaps the dog.

JAMIE WYETH

Did you ever stop to think that a dog is the only animal that doesn't have to work for a living? A hen has to lay eggs; a cow has to give milk; and a canary has to sing. But a dog makes his living by giving you nothing but love.

DALE CARNEGIE, *How to Win Friends and Influence People*

Pets can be considered to manipulate the human species. They are similar in this regard to social parasites such as the cuckoo. . . The affection, food and time and energy devoted to a pet is not repaid in terms of related offspring and it could have been more profitably spent caring for human offspring and relatives.

JOHN ARCHER, *The Nature of Grief*

The dog commends himself to our favour by affording play to our propensity for mastery, and as he is also an item of expense, and commonly serves no industrial purpose, he holds a well-assured place in men's regard as a thing of good repute.

THORSTEIN VEBLEN, *The Theory of the Leisure Class*

He could steal and forage to perfection; he had an instinct that was positively gruesome for divining when work was to be done and for making a sneak accordingly; and for getting lost and not staying lost was nothing short of inspired. But when it came to work, the way that intelligence dribbled out of him and left him a mere clot of wobbling, stupid jelly would make your heart bleed.

JACK LONDON, "That Spot."

For my therapy dog, specifically, and for therapy dogs in general, giving and receiving love was as much a vocation as herding was to a border collie. And the thing was, like the best love, it was antiphonal, a call and response that grew louder over time, even some of the voices were fading.

SUE HALPERN, *A Dog Walks into a Nursing Home*

The early walk up the hill had become a ritual for me in West Hebron – navigating the steep and rocky rise with the dogs to watch the sun appear. Was there any finer way to start a day?

JON KATZ, *The Dogs of Bedlam Farm*

Dogs are our link to paradise. They don't know evil or jealousy or discontent. To sit with a dog on a hillside on a glorious afternoon is to be back in Eden, where doing nothing was not boring – it was peace.

MILAN KUNDERA, *The Unbearable Lightness of Being*

Arnold was a dog's dog. Whenever he shuffled along walks or through alleyways, he always gave the impression of being onto something big.

MARTHA GRIMES, *The Old Fox Deceiv'd*

There is a hope that a dog injects into every walk. More than a hope – an expectation, really – that this is going to be something wonderful.

JOHN ZEAMAN, *Dog Walks Man*

Dogs, with their nose-to-the-ground, tail-wagging eagerness, their let-me-at-that-squirrel enthusiasm, remind me that what may on some days seem routine and dreary is only that way if you refuse to see the world at each moment with new eyes.

STEVEN BAUER, *Dogs We Love*

You should see my corgis at sunset in the snow. It's their finest hour About five o'clock they glow like copper. Then they come in and lie in front of the fire like a string of sausages.

TASHA TUDOR, *The Private World of Tasha Tudor*

Of course what he most intensely dreams of is being taken out on walks, and the more you are able to indulge him the more will he adore you and the more all the latent beauty of his nature will come out.

HENRY JAMES, quoted in *A Dog at All Things*, by Agnes Lauchlan

Dogs are like [philosopher Immanuel] Kant who always want to take the same walk. The less it changes, the happier they are.
ROGER GRENIER, *The Difficulty of Being a Dog*

I took my dog for a walk. . . all the way from New York to Florida. I said to him, "There, now you're done."
STEVEN WRIGHT

I wish I could vanish into my hound as he goes through these woods, looking up at the branches in the sunlight, the leaves falling on him.
ANDREW WYETH

Walking a dog
you meet
Lots of dogs.
SOCHI

When we get home, Jacques is likely to nuzzle my hand before we go about our individual tasks. (Usually I go to my desk and Jacques to his couch, for another of the naps in which he specializes.) If I didn't know better, I'd take him to be saying, "Great walk, Boss!"
DANIEL PINKWATER, *Dogs We Love*

Every day, the dog and I, go for a tramp in the woods. And he loves it! Mind you, the tramp is getting a bit fed up.
JERRY DENNIS, American naturalist author

I thought a long time about my dog Black Dog and what the two winters must have been when he had no master in Ketchum, Idaho, having been lost or abandoned by some summer motorist. Any small hardships we had encountered seemed to me to be dwarfed by Blackie's odyssey.

ERNEST HEMINGWAY, "The Christmas Gift"

Like pigeons, dogs are thought to have a supernatural ability to find their way home across hundreds, even thousands, of miles of strange terrain. The newspapers are full of stories of dogs who have miraculously turned up at the doorsteps of baffled masters who had abandoned them afar. Against these stories can be set the lost and found columns of the same papers, which in almost every issue carry offers of rewards for the recovery of dogs that, apparently, couldn't find their way back from the next block.

BERGEN EVANS, *The Natural History of Nonsense*

If I sit down on a bench he is at my side at once and takes up a position on one of my feet. For it is a law of his being that he only runs about when I am in motion too; that when I settle down he follows suit.

THOMAS MANN, "A Man and His Dog"

In the streets of New York between seven and nine in the morning you will see the slow procession of dog and owner proceeding from street to tree to hydrant to trash basket. They are apartment dogs. They are taken out twice a day, and, while it is a cliche, it is truly amazing how owner and dog resemble one another. They grow to walk alike, have the same set of head.

JOHN STEINBECK, quoted in *Cold Noses and Warm Hearts*, edited by Corey Ford

I just bought a Chihuahua. It is the dog for lazy people. You don't have to walk it. Just hold it out the window and squeeze.

ANTHONY CLARK

Never stand between a dog and the hydrant.

JOHN PEERS, *1,001 Logical Laws, Accurate Axioms, Profound Principles, Trusty Truisms*

Dogs read the world through their noses, and write their history in urine.

J.R. ACKERLEY, *My Dog Tulip*

Dogs need to sniff the ground; it's how they keep abreast of current events. The ground is a giant dog newspaper, containing all kinds of late-breaking dog news items, which, if they are especially urgent, are often continued in the next yard.

DAVE BARRY

It is my experience that in some areas Charley is more intelligent than I am, but in others he is abysmally ignorant. He can't read, can't drive a car, and has no grasp of mathematics. But in his own field of endeavor, which he is now practicing, the slow imperial smelling over and anointing an area, he has no peer. Of course, his horizons are limited, but how wide are mine.

JOHN STEINBECK, *Travels With Charley*

Some of our greatest historical and artistic treasures we place in museums; others, we take for walks.

ROGER CARAS

You know that you are superior to me, physically. I may be able to throw a Frisbee, but you can chew one up. I can hurl a tennis ball down the street, but you can catch it in midair and then soak it in saliva so that I won't want to touch it. And you can run faster. I will never catch you.

BRUCE CAMERON, "A Dog Day of Summer"

You could not divert her attention from a ball by making loud noises, calling her name, or even offering her food. Given the choice between eating her dinner and fetching a ball, Amber will always go for the ball – and that is saying something, because she has been clocked at forty-two seconds downing her kibble.

JANE SMILEY, *Dogs We Love*

There are two things that won't last long in this world, and that's dogs chasing cars and pros putting for pars.

LEE TREVINO, golfer

He took off at full throttle, racing around the yard in a series of giant, loping leaps interrupted every few seconds by a random somersault or nosedive. Snow was almost as much fun as raiding the neighbor's trash.

JOHN GROGAN, *Marley and Me*

Sophie was a great teacher – nothing kept her down. She was literally unsinkable. On the beach she dove for rocks and swam out for sticks. The sticks were almost too easy for her, a toss, a splash, a paddle: "Here's your stick back, Bill." The rocks were more interesting. I'd sail them out twenty feet or more, and she'd dive to the bottom, root through other stones down there, and return with the precise rock thrown.

BILL HENDERSON, *All My Dogs*

Swimming with Marley was a potentially life threatening adventure, a little like swimming with an ocean liner. He would come at you full speed ahead, his paws flailing out in front of him. You'd expect him to veer away at the last minute, but he would simply crash into you and attempt to climb aboard. If you were over your head he simply pushed you beneath the surface.

JOHN GROGAN, *Marley and Me*

The most affectionate creature in the world is a wet dog.

AMBROSE BIERCE, *Collected Works*

He had as much fun in the water as any person I have known. You didn't have to throw a stick in the water to get him to go in. Of course, he would bring back a stick if you did throw one in. He would even have brought back a piano if you had thrown one in.

JAMES THURBER, on his dog Rex. *Thurber's Dogs*

I'm a detective and expecting me to run criminals down and then let them go free is like asking a dog to catch a rabbit and then let it go. It can be done, all right, and sometimes it is done, but it's not the natural thing.

SAM SPADE, *The Maltese Falcon*, by DASHIELL HAMMETT

His life's mission was to catch one of the countless rabbits that considered my garden their own personal salad bar. He would spot a rabbit munching the lettuce and barrel off down the hill in hot pursuit, ears flapping behind him, paws pounding the ground, his bark filling the air. He was about as stealthy as a marching band and never got closer than a dozen feet before his intended prey scampered off into the woods and safety.

 JOHN GROGAN, *Marley and Me*

Take a crosscut saw coon hunting with you. When you tree a coon, hold the dog and cut the tree down, or either climb the tree and make the coon jump in amongst the dogs. Give him a sporting chance.

 JERRY CLOWER, "A Coon Huntin' Story"

He was just as happy as a dog could be, and perhaps he was proud of the wound that left a straight line from his shoulder to his hip, and showed up like a cord under the golden brindle as long as he lived – a memento of his first real hunt.

 JAMES PERCY FITZPATRICK, *Jock of the Bushveld*

That dog won't hunt.

 ANN RICHARDS, keynote speech at the 1988 Democratic Convention

House Dogs

A house is not a home until it has a dog.
  GERALD DURRELL

Furniture looks more comfortable when there's a dog on
it.
  CATHERINE CHARLTON, *Crockern Farm Journals*

These are the simple rules. No barking, no growling, you
will not lift you leg to anything in this house. This is not
your room. No slobbering, no chewing, you will wear a
flea collar. This is not your room. No begging for food, no
sniffing of crotches, and you will not drink from my toilet.
This is not your room.
  TOM HANKS, instructing the dog Hooch,
  in *Turner and Hooch*

To a dog, the Bed is an amazing invention, perhaps the most perfect, and certainly the most useful ever devised by humans. The top of the bed allows the dog to stretch out in any direction he wishes. He can shift his position freely; in daytime he can find the sunniest spot. If the temperature is below the required level, it is possible to throw the bedspread on the floor and get under the blanket.

STEPHEN BAKER, *How to Live With a Neurotic Dog*

You sleep before, and after, every meal.
Things would be said
If I had so much bed.

A.P. HERBERT

No animal should ever jump on the dining-room furniture unless absolutely certain that he can hold his own in conversation.

FRAN LEBOWITZ, *Social Studies*

Only when you love dogs very much do you let them sit on $300-per-yard French fabric. I am the Angelina Jolie of barkers.

JOAN RIVERS

Our house was always filled with dogs. . . . They helped make our house a kennel, it is true, but the constant patter of their filthy paws and the dreadful result of their brainless activities have warmed me throughout the years.

HELEN HAYES, *On Reflection*

At night my wife and I did fall about the dog's being put down in the cellar, which I had a mind to have done because of his fouling the house, and I would have my will; and so we went to bed and lay all night in a quarrel.

SAMUEL PEPYS, *Diary of Samuel Pepys*

Reluctantly, I have come to accept the fact that on certain stormy nights our forty-five pound dog, overwhelmed by fear, will triumph over a pair of gimpy knees, jackknife into the air, and crash-land onto the tall bed that my wife Jessica and I share—scaring the absolute bejesus out of me.

DEAN KING, "The Girls Club"

Over the years, Murphy had expanded his personal mattress territory by snuggling into the valley of comforter between me and my husband, then bracing his back against me, his feet against Larry, and slooowly stretching out his legs and locking his knees. Blanketless, we shivered and clung to the edges, sleeping fitfully between bouts of canine kickboxing and snoring.

BETH KENDRICK, "Are You Smarter Than a Terrier"

Every dog should have a man of his own. There is nothing like a well-behaved person around the house to spread the dog's blanket for him, or bring him supper when he comes home man-tired at night.

COREY FORD, *Every Dog Should Have A Man*

My dog is not afraid of grizzly bears, but the vacuum scares the crap out of him. He won't eat broccoli, but he'll happily feast on dried cat turds. He trembles in fear if he sees me holding a bottle of dog shampoo, but he'd fearlessly sprint across the freeway if there was a squirrel on the other side.

THE OATMEAL AND MATTHEW INMAN,
My Dog: The Paradox

Anyone who doesn't know what soap tastes like never washed a dog.

FRANKLIN P. JONES

When showering with your dog it is advisable to wear swim wear. I don't know if your dog would know if you were naked, but you would know.

MERRILL MARKOE, *What The Dogs Have Taught Me*

A door is what a dog is perpetually on the wrong side of.

OGDEN NASH, "A Dog's Best Friend is his Illiteracy"

I wonder what goes through his mind when he sees us peeing in his water bowl.

PENNY WARD MOSER, *Sniff Seattle*

There were days I swore that if I lit a match the whole house would go up. Marley was able to clear an entire room with his silent, deadly flatulence, which seemed to increase in direct correlation to the number of dinner guests we had in our home.

JOHN GROGAN, *Marley and Me*

Ladies and gentlemen are permitted to have friends in the kennel, but not in the kitchen.

GEORGE BERNARD SHAW

We are alone, absolutely alone on this chance planet: and, amid all the forms of life that surround us, not one, excepting the dog has made an alliance with us.

MAURICE MAETERLINCK, *Our Friend, the Dog*

Human beings wind up having the relationship with dogs that they fool themselves they will have with other people. When we are very young, it is the perfect communion we honestly believe we will have with a lover; when we are older, it is the symbiosis we manage to fool ourselves we will always have with our children.

ANNA QUINDLEN, *Good Dog. Stay.*

He who is cruel to animals becomes hard also in his dealings with men. We can judge the heart of a man by his treatment of animals.

IMMANUEL KANT

"A man can't be all bad when he is kind to dogs." That is what they generally always say and that is the reason you see so many men stop on the st. (sic) when they see a dog and pet it because they figure that maybe somebody will looking at him will do it, and the next time they are getting panned, why who ever seen it will speak up and say: "He can't be all bad because he likes dogs."

RING LARDNER, *Dogs*

If a dog will not come to you after he has looked you in the face, you ought to go home and examine your conscience.

WOODROW WILSON

When a man's dog turns against him it is time for a wife to pack her trunk and go home to mama.

MARK TWAIN

From the dog's point of view his master is an elongated and abnormally cunning dog.
MABEL LOUISE ROBINSON

I don't see dogs as psychic or telepathic. Nor do I believe that we will meet them in the afterlife, or that mediums can channel their deepest thoughts. But I do believe that the human-dog relationship can be deeply meaningful. Dogs have a remarkable gift for entering our lives at particular times and weaving themselves in. It is one of their most endearing traits, a key part of their impressive adaptability.
JON KATZ, *The Dogs of Bedlam Farm*

I have found that when you are deeply troubled there are things that you get from the silent devoted companionship of a dog that you can get from no other source.
DORIS DAY, *Doris Day: Her Own Story*

The world was conquered through the understanding of dogs; the world exists through the understanding of dogs.
NIETZCHE

All knowledge, the totality of all questions and all answers is contained in the dog.
FRANZ KAFKA, "Investigations of a Dog."

Recollect that the Almighty, who gave the dog to be companion of our pleasures and our toils, hath invested him with a nature noble and incapable of deceit.
SIR WALTER SCOTT, *The Talisman*

Dogs are blameless, devoid of calculation, neither blessed nor cursed with human motives. They can't really be held responsible for what they do. But we can.

JON KATZ, *The Dogs of Bedlam Farm*

If you eliminate smoking and gambling, you will be amazed to find that almost all an Englishman's pleasures can be, and mostly are, shared by his dog.

GEORGE BERNARD SHAW

There's facts about dogs, and then there's opinions about them. The dogs have the facts, and the humans have the opinions. If you want the facts about the dog, always get them straight from the dog. If you want opinions, get them from humans.

J. ALLEN BOONE, *Kinship With all Life*

The great pleasure of a dog is that you may make a fool of yourself with him and not only will he not scold you, he will make a fool of himself, too.

SAMUEL BUTLER, *The Notebooks of Samuel Butler*

Dogs act exactly the way we would act if we had no shame.

CYNTHIA HEIMEL, *Get Your Tongue Out of My Mouth, I'm Kissing You Good-bye!*

The Dog Wish . . . the strange and involved compulsion to be as happy and carefree as a dog.

JAMES THURBER, *Thurber's Dogs*

I think we are drawn to dogs because they are the uninhibited creatures we might be if we weren't certain we knew better.

GEORGE BIRD EVANS, *Troubles with Bird Dogs, and What to Do about Them*

A dog will make eye contact. A cat will, too, but a cat's eyes don't look entirely warm-blooded to me, whereas a dog's eyes look human except less guarded. A dog will look at you as if to say, "What do you want me to do for you? I'll do anything for you." Whether a dog can in fact, do anything for you if you don't have sheep (I never have) is another matter. A dog is willing.

ROY BLOUNT, Jr., *Now, Where Were We?*

I am convinced that some dogs, like some people, are corrupted by prosperity. I don't know why, but perhaps it involves some quality in the moral fiber.

HAL BORLAND, *The Dog Who Came to Stay*

On the other hand I distrust people who believe that dogs are better than we are. Dogs are not better. They are just different from us. Surely they can do some things better, but I have yet to see a dog balance a checkbook or make an omelet or compose a sonnet.

JOHN STEINBECK, quoted in *A Thinking Dog's Man,*
by Ted Patrick

{ *Love a Dog* }

Therefore to this dog will I,
Tenderly not scornfully,
Render praise and favor. . . .
ELIZABETH BARRETT BROWNING,
"To Flush, My Dog"

I have always thought of a dog lover as a dog that was in
love with another dog.
JAMES THURBER

There is no doubt about it. Dog loving is closely associated
to the pounding-yourself-on-the-head- with-a-hammer-
because-it-is-so-pleasant-when-you-stop school of mas-
ochism.
BETTY MACDONALD, *Onions in the Stew*

Dog. A kind of additional or subsidiary Diety designed to
catch the overflow and surplus of the world's worship.
AMBROSE BIERCE, *The Devil's Dictionary*

You said "must love dogs," not "must own dogs."
I do love dogs.
In fact, I had one with my ex. She was allergic, went into
anaphylactic shock. So we had to put her down.
Dog. Not the wife.
I'm kidding about both.
    JOHN CUSACK, in *Must Love Dogs*

I never formed an attachment to dogs when I was young.
I was, the truth be told, a little bit afraid of them. Perhaps
that helps explains the passion with which I embrace all
things canine now in middle age.
    JOSEPH DUEMER, *Dog Music*

I could discern clearly, even at that early age, the essential difference between people who are kind to dogs and
people who really love them.
    FRANCES P. COBBE, *The Confessions of a Lost Dog*

The plain fact that my dog loves me more than I love him
is undeniable and always fills me with a certain feeling of
shame. The dog is very ready to lay down his life for me.
    KONRAD LORENZ

A dog's need for reassurance is a bottomless well. You
could devote an entire day to ministering to a dog's need
to feel wanted – stroking it, romping with it, crooning
over it – and the instant you desisted, the rejected creature
with an imploring whimper, would nose under your arm
to confront you with an expression of bewilderment and

hurt. Don't you love me anymore? its eyes would ask. Am
I hateful to you? Do you wish I were dead?
  CHARLTON OGBURN, JR.

Most dogs have this idea running through their minds
constantly: "Petme petme petme petme petme."
  BETTY FISHER & SUZANNE DELZIO,
  So Your Dog's Not Lassie

We might speak harshly or show our annoyance at our
dogs, but they are forever forgiving. Even at the most un-
expected moments, they will sidle up to you and and push
their moist nostrils at your face as if to say they are forever
sorry, and you are their loving master who they will always
love.
  SIR DAVID TANG, *Financial Times*

I marvel that such small ribs as these can cage such vast
desire to please.
  OGDEN NASH, "Please Pass The Biscuit"

My little dog: a heartbeat at my feet.
  EDITH WHARTON, "A Lyrical Epigram"

Whoever loveth me, loveth my hound.
  SIR THOMAS MORE

Qui me amat, amat et canem meum (Who loves me, also
loves my dog)
  SAINT BERNARD OF CLAIRVAUX

The time comes to every dog when it ceases to care for people merely for biscuits or bones, or even for caresses, and walks out of doors. When a dog really loves, it prefers the person who gives it nothing, or perhaps is too ill ever to take it out for exercise, to all the liberal cooks and active dog-boys in the world.

FRANCES P. COBBE, *The Confessions of a Lost Dog*

Man is dog's ideal of what God should be.

HOLBROOK JACKSON, *Platitudes in the Making*

A dog needs God. It lives by your glances your wishes. It even shares your humor. This happens about the fifth year. If it doesn't happen you are only keeping an animal.

ENID BAGNOLD, *Enid Bagnold's Autobiography*

To his dog, every man is Napoleon; hence, the constant popularity of dogs.

ALDOUS HUXLEY

If your dog thinks you're the greatest person in the world, don't seek a second opinion.

JIM FIEBIG, American author

Know yourself. Don't accept your dog's admiration as conclusive evidence that you are wonderful.

ANN LANDERS

I got into the habit of turning the bathtub faucet on at a trickle while I was in the bathroom so Marley could lap up some cool, fresh water. The dog could not have been more thrilled had I built him an exact replica of Splash Mountain.

JOHN GROGAN, *Marley and Me*

A dog is the only thing on this earth that loves you more than he loves himself.

JOSH BILLINGS, *Josh Billings' Sayings*

Dogs are not our whole life, but they make our lives whole.

ROGER CARAS

Dogs have given us their absolute all. We are the center of their universe. We are the focus of their love and faith and trust. They serve us in return for scraps. It is without a doubt the best deal man has ever made.

ROGER CARAS

One of the most beautiful things in human experience is a sense of poignancy, and I never fail to find it in the companionship of a dog. In this animal which, rightly or wrongly, we have come to domesticate, we have created a very special kind of camaraderie. It is special because the dog gives up love unconditionally.

SIR DAVID TANG

And then there are those special times when he leans over to nuzzle me with his snout—which I always take to be an incredibly moving tribute to the amazing bond that our species are able to share... until I remember, too late, that most of the times he does this he is simply looking for a cozy place to throw up.

MERRILL MARKOE, *What The Dogs Have Taught Me*

He may look just the same to you,
and he may be just as fine,
But the next-door dog is the next-door dog,
And mine—is—mine!

DIXIE WILLSON, "Next Door Dog"

Dogs Are Better

Dogs are better than human beings, because they know and do not tell.
  EMILY DICKINSON

The more I see of the representatives of the people, the more I admire my dogs.
  ALPHONSE DE LAMARTINE

The more I see of men, the more I like dogs.
  MADAME DE STAEL

The average dog is a nicer person than the average person.
  ANDY ROONEY

The humans have tried everything. Now it's up to us dogs.
   DANNY, in *101 Dalmations*

Man is an animal that makes bargains; no other animal
does this – one dog does not change a bone with another.
   ADAM SMITH

On the internet, nobody knows you're a dog.
   PETER STEINER, cartoon caption

I like dogs better [than people]. They give you uncondi-
tional love. They either lick your face or bite you, but you
always know where they're coming from. With people, you
never know which ones will bite. The difference between
dogs and men is that you know where dogs sleep at night.
   GREG LOUGANIS, Olympic athlete

If poodles, who walk so easily on their hind legs, ever do
learn the little tricks of speech and reason, I should not be
surprised if they made a better job of it than Man, who
would seem to be surely but not slowly slipping back to
all fours.
   JAMES THURBER, a memorial to his dog Medve,
   PM Magazine

Dogs love their friends and bite their enemies, quite unlike
people, who are incapable of pure love and have to mix
love and hate.
   SIGMUND FREUD, in a letter to his friend
   Marie Bonaparte.

The advantages of whiskey over dogs are legion. Whiskey does not need to be periodically wormed, it does not need to be fed, it never requires a special kennel, it has no toenails to be clipped or coat to be stripped. Whiskey sits quietly on its special nook until you want it. True, whiskey has a nasty habit of running out, but then so does a dog.

W.C. FIELDS, *W.C. Fields By Himself*

Shows & Clothes

And to think that in some countries these dogs are eaten.
FRED WILLARD as BUCK LAUGHLIN, in *Best in Show*

There are dogs you've never seen before back here, there are dogs you've never heard of before. And there is a certain snootiness. Pomeranians speak only to poodles, and poodles speak only to God.
CHARLES KURALT, at the Westminster Dog Show

I wasn't paranoid; there were cliques among the dog people in the park. And cliques among the dogs. There were dogs who didn't get along and people who didn't get along, unrelated to how the canines felt. There were grudges going back years, usually involving stolen toys or balls or perceived slights.

LOUISE BERNIKOW, *Bark If You Love Me*

Dogs of uncertain pedigree are often made to feel socially inferior. Pure ancestry assures entree to dog shows, while doors are closed to the most numerous and perhaps most successful breed of all: the mutt.

STEPHEN BAKER, *How to Live With a Neurotic Dog*

Dogs, the foremost snobs in creation, are quick to notice the difference between a well-clad and a disreputable stranger.

ALBERT PAYSON TERHUNE, *Further Adventures of Lad*

I love to talk to the trainers, the handlers, the owners, and different things intrigue me: why a guy would buy a $900 suit and put four pounds of calf liver in his pocket to feed the dog. That always is intriguing to me.

JOE GARAGIOLA, announcing at the Westminster Dog Show

Just as I am unable to think of any great intellectul who physically approaches anywhere near to an Adonis, or a really beautiful woman who is even tolerably intelligent, in the same way I know of no "champion" of any dog breed which I should ever wish to own myself.

KONRAD LORENZ, *Man Meets Dog*

I would rather see the portrait of a dog that I know, than all the allegorical paintings they can show me in the world.

SAMUEL JOHNSON

Now tell me, which one of these dogs would you want to have as your wide receiver on your football team?

FRED WILLARD as BUCK LAUGHLIN, in *Best in Show*

Show business is dog eat dog. It's worse than dog eat dog. It's dog doesn't return dog's phone calls.

WOODY ALLEN

"I have this fantasy where I look out, and the whole audience is dogs." "Are you kidding? I have the same fantasy."

LAURIE ANDERSON to YO-YO MA

Dear Mr Jennings: Many thanks for your kindness in making me a member of Euclid Kennel Club. You will go to your grave never knowing how I appreciate the favor.

FRED ALLEN, in a letter to Herb Jennings,
October 10, 1929

From a pedigree yellow pup I grew up to be an anonymous yellow cur looking like a cross between an Angora cat and a box of lemons. But my mistress never tumbled. She thought that the two primeval pups that Noah chased into the ark were but a collateral branch of my ancestors. It took two policemen to keep her from entering me at the Madison Square Garden for the Siberian bloodhound prize.

O. HENRY, *The Four Million*

Look at Scott! He is prancing along with the dog! Man, I tell you something, if you live in my neighborhood and you're dressed like that, you'd better be a hotel doorman.

FRED WILLARD as BUCK LAUGHLIN, in *Best in Show*

For centuries dogs ran around naked. Modern civilization put an end to all that. Today, thanks to man's thoughtfulness, there is clothing to fit every dog, no matter what the dog's girth, height or budget.

STEPHEN BAKER, *How to Live With a Neurotic Dog*

Dogs are not a child substitute, dogs are not a man substitute, dogs are a shopping substitute.

CYNTHIA HEIMEL

A dog has no use for fancy cars or big homes or designer clothes. Status symbols mean nothing to him. A waterlogged stick will do just fine.

JOHN GROGAN, *Marley and Me*

You know why dogs have no money? No pockets. They see change on the street all the time and it drives them crazy. There's nothing they can do about it. "There's a quarter. I could've used that."

JERRY SEINFELD

In late September, I sat with Otto on our couch and we began the process of finding him a Halloween costume. I knew he had no idea what was going on, but my enthusiasm was enough to make him know he was going to hate it.

JULIE KLAM, *You had Me at Woof*

There is no excuse for pampering, constant fondling, dressing up in clothing and other ridiculous customs. Dogs should be treated like the animals they are.

A. HYATT VERRILL, *Pets For Pleasure and Profit (1915)*

If you are a dog and your owner suggests that you should wear a sweater... suggest that he wear a tail.

FRAN LEBOWITZ, *Social Studies*

Better a sweater from a dog you know and love, than from a sheep you never met.

KENDALL CROLIUS, *Knitting With Dog Hair*

All dogs are fascinated by clothing – yours, mine, the girl-next door's. While they may seem to jump up in an apparently joyful, unrestrained show of greeting or affection, they really want to feel fabric, any fabric. To try and break them of this habit is to deprive them of a very sensuous experience.

DANNY SHANAHAN, *Dogs We Love*

There is another reason for dressing well, namely that dogs respect it and will not attack you in good clothes.

RALPH WALDO EMERSON

Presidents & Kings

If you want a friend in Washington, get a dog.
  HARRY TRUMAN

Any man who does not like dogs and want them about
does not deserve to be in the White House.
  CALVIN COOLIDGE

Jesse has a new dog. You may have noticed that his former pets have been peculiarly unfortunate. When this dog dies every employee in the White House will be at once discharged.

ULYSSES GRANT, to the White House staff when his son got a Newfoundland puppy. The previous dogs had all died mysteriously.

When it comes to persuading the electorate, there is currently nothing more important to a candidate than a wife, kids, and the right kind of animals. Dogs are a great asset to candidates, and the feeling seems to be engendered that if a dog loves the candidate, he can't be all that bad.

DICK GREGORY

To make them bark. It's good for them.

LYNDON B. JOHNSON explaining why he picked up his beagles by their ears.

President Lyndon B. Johnson used to lift his dogs by the ears – the dog's ears. Eventually he tore the ears off, but that didn't matter much: the dog never came when it was called.

VICTOR BORGE

Politics are not my concern. . . they impressed me as a dog's life without a dog's decencies.

RUDYARD KIPLING

Politicians are interested in People. Now that is not always a virtue. Dogs are interested in fleas.
    P.J. O'ROURKE, *Parliament of Whores*

America is a large friendly dog in a small room. Every time it wags it's tail it knocks over a chair.
    ARNOLD TOYNBEE

Study hard, and you might grow up to be President. But let's face it: even then, you'll never make as much money as your dog.
    GEORGE H. W. BUSH, 1992 speech to graduates after
    learning Millie, his dog, made $889,176 in
    book royalties.

I love a dog. He does nothing for political reasons.
    WILL ROGERS, *The Best of Will Rogers*

One other thing I probably should tell you because if we don't they'll probably be saying this about me too, we did get something – a gift – after the election. A man down in Texas heard Pat on the radio mention the fact that our two youngsters would like to have a dog. And, believe it or not, the day before we left on this campaign trip we got a message from Union Station in Baltimore saying they had a package for us. We went down to get it. You know what it was? It was a little cocker spaniel dog in a crate that he'd sent all the way from Texas. Black and white spotted. And our little girl – Tricia, the 6-year-old – named it Checkers. And you know, the kids, like all kids, love the dog and I just want to say this right now, that regardless of what they say about it, we're gonna keep it.

> RICHARD M. NIXON, in his famous "Checkers" speech, September 23, 1952. It was seen by 60 million viewers, the largest television audience up to that time.

[My dog] can bark like a congressman, fetch like an aide, beg like a press secretary and play dead like a receptionist when the phone rings.

> GERALD SOLOMON, New York Congressman

If ever the world's diplomats and arms negotiators learn the spaniel's gaze, there will be peace on earth.

> LARRY SHOOK, *The Puppy Report*

These Republican leaders have not been content with attacks on me, or my wife, or on my sons. No, not content with that, they now include my little dog, Fala. Well, of course, I don't resent attacks, and my family don't resent attacks, but Fala does resent them. You know, Fala is Scotch, and being a Scottie, as soon as he learned that the Republican fiction writers in Congress and out had concocted a story that I'd left him behind on the Aleutian Islands and had sent a destroyer back to find him – at a cost to the taxpayers of two or three, or eight or twenty million dollars – his Scotch soul was furious. He has not been the same dog since. I am accustomed to hearing malicious falsehoods about myself. . . . But I think I have a right to resent, to object, to libelous statements about my dog!

> FRANKLIN D. ROOSEVELT

Minutes after FDR died ". . . a snapping, snarling series of barks was heard. No one had paid any attention to Fala. He had been dozing in a corner of the room. For a reason beyond understanding, he ran directly for the front screen door and bashed his black head against it. The screen broke and he crawled through and ran snapping and barking up into the hills. There, Secret Service men could see him, standing alone, unmoving, on an eminence. This led to the quiet question: 'Do dogs really know?'"

    JIM BISHOP, *FDR's Last Year*

"My mother told a funny story," said Caroline Kennedy, the US ambassador to Japan. "She was sitting next to Khrushchev at a state dinner in Vienna. She ran out of things to talk about, so she asked about the dog, Strelka, that the Russians had shot into space. During the conversation, my mother asked about Strelka's puppies. A few months later, a puppy arrived and my father had no idea where the dog came from and couldn't believe my mother had done that." The puppy was Strelka's daughter, Pushinka, listed on her official registration certificate as a "non-breed" or mongrel. "Pushinka was cute and fluffy," noted Ambassador Kennedy. The Russian name translates as Fluffy.

    Told by ALISON GEE, of BBC

I am His Highness' dog at Kew. Pray tell me sir, whose dog are you?

    ALEXANDER POPE, noting the collar of a dog given to Frederick, Prince of Wales.

QUEEN ELIZABETH was once asked how, given the different heights, Corgis and Dachshunds were able to mate. "It's very simple. We have a little brick."

I dressed dear sweet little Dash for the second time after dinner in a scarlet jacket and blue trousers.

QUEEN VICTORIA, on her Cavalier King Charles spaniel. On the day the young Victoria was crowned queen at age 18, she came home and gave Dash a bath.

Old Dogs

It's hard to teach an old dog new tricks.
UNKNOWN

The old saw about old dogs and new tricks only applies to certain people.
DANIEL PINKWATER, *Train Your Dog, Dammit!*

I can't think of anything that brings me closer to tears than when my old dog – completely exhausted after a hard day in the field – limps away from her nice spot in front of the fire and comes over to where I'm sitting and puts her head in my lap, a paw over my knee, and closes her eyes and goes back to sleep. I don't know what I've done to deserve that kind of friend.
GENE HILL, "The Dog Man"

As we watched him grow gray and deaf and creaky, there was no ignoring his mortality – or ours. Age sneaks up on us all, but it sneaks up on a dog with a swiftness that is both breathtaking and sobering.

JOHN GROGAN, *Marley and Me*

Blessed is the person who has earned the love of an old dog.

SYDNEY JEANNE SEWARD

Old dogs, like old shoes, are comfortable. They might be a bit out of shape and a little worn around the edges, but they fit well.

BONNIE WILCOX, *Old Dogs, Old Friends*

A puppy plays with every pup he meets, but an old dog has few associates.

JOSH BILLINGS, *Josh Billings' Sayings*

The old dog stood very erect and proud, his tail waving slowly. He always took it as a tremendous compliment when I examined him and there was no doubt he was enjoying himself now. Straightening up, I patted his head, and he responded immediately by trying to put his paws on my chest.

JAMES HERRIOT, *Favorite Dog Stories*

There are three faithful friends – an old wife, an old dog, and ready money.

BENJAMIN FRANKLIN, *Poor Richard's Almanack*

Marley reminded me of life's brevity, of its fleeting joys and missed opportunities. He reminded me that each of us gets one shot at the gold, with no replays. One day you are swimming halfway out into the ocean convinced that this will be the day you will catch that seagull: the next you're barely able to bend down and drink out of your water bowl.

JOHN GROGAN, *Marley and Me*

Having an old dog and watching her have the grace to just slow down and spend more time in the sun, it was an experience I would never have wanted to miss. It was, in many ways, a way that we learned about death and how to get old, and how to do it, and how to be there and not just pretend it wasn't happening.

LAURIE ANDERSON, talking about her dog Lollabelle in *Heart Of A Dog*

Dogs come into our lives to teach us about love. . . . they depart to teach us about loss. A new dog never replaces an old dog; it merely expands the heart. If you have loved many dogs, your heart is very big.

ERICA JONG

Pete outlived Tibor. He came with me when I went to visit Tibor's grave. Sat under the tree. Watched me weep, saying not a word. And then, in a few years, it was Pete's turn to die. And I held him and said goodbye. I have not been able to replace Pete. Because he holds my heart. Or because I am selfish and don't want to think about walking a dog. Or I travel so much. Or I want my shoes unchewed. Or because the children are now grown and live in their own homes. Or because I am afraid of a broken heart.

MAIRA KALMAN

I swear he figured out how to use his deafness to his advantage. Drop a piece of steak in his bowl, and he would come trotting in from the next room. He still had the ability to detect the dull, satisfying thud of meat on metal. But yell for him to come when he had somewhere else he'd rather be going, and he'd stroll blithely away from you.

JOHN GROGAN, *Marley and Me*

There came a time when a scrap thrown in his direction usually bounced unseen off his head. Yet put a pork roast in the oven, and the guy still breathed as audibly as an obscene caller. The eyes and ears may have gone, but the nose was eternal. And the tail. The tail still wagged, albeit at half mast. When it stops, I thought more than once, then we'll know.

Anna Quindlen, on her aging dog Beau.
Good Dog. Stay.

When did any dog turn up his nose at a smell. . . .Times are, indeed, when smelliness pure and simple, quantity rather than quality, join the ineffable affluence of Nature's bounty to the nose, seems to ravish one of those great lovers almost clean off the earth.

C.E. Montague, *The Right Place*

All Good Dogs Go to Heaven

If a man shall meet a Black Dog once, it shall be for joy; and if twice, it shall be for sorrow; and a third time, he shall die.

AMERICAN LEGEND

Britain and the United States have extensive black dog myths – the black dog is supernatural, huge, with glowing eyes. If you happen to see it, start to make your arrangements, because you're toast.

JOHN HOMANS, *What's a Dog For?*

In dog years I'm dead.

UNKNOWN

Animals have these advantages over man: they never hear the clock strike, they die without any idea of death, they have no theologists to instruct them, their last moments are not disturbed by unwelcome and unpleasant ceremonies, their funerals cost them nothing, and no one starts law suits over their wills.

VOLTAIRE

In a dog's life
A year is really more like seven
And all too soon a canine
Will be chasing cars in doggie heaven.

LYRIC FROM RUSH

Dogs' lives are too short. Their only fault, really.

AGNES TURNBULL, *The Flowering*

Sometimes it seems the whole purpose of pets is to bring death into the house.

JOHN UPDIKE

The life of a good dog is like the life of a good person, only shorter and more compressed.

ANNA QUINDLEN, *Good Dog. Stay.*

If you live a good life, you get to come back as a gay couple's dog. Trust me, Mother Teresa is a Shih Tzu living on the Upper East Side wearing a Dolce & Gabanna trench coat and having her crap picked up by Uncle Steve and Uncle Dave.

ALEC MAPA, "There's No Place Like Home, Judy"

I guess you don't really own a dog, you rent them, and you have to be thankful that you had a long lease.

JOE GARAGIOLA

Since dogs are relatively unimportant in the adult world, it is probably foolish to grieve when they go. But most people do grieve, inconsolably, for a time, and feel restless, lonely and poor.

BROOKS ATKINSON, *Cold Noses and Warm Hearts*

Yet, Hot seemed to be saying to me, 'Don't worry, Master, I have had a good life, and you have given me a good life, and I am sorry for all the little faults that I have had. But you have been my master and I am glad that I have been able to make you happy at times. When I am in heaven, I will remain faithful to you in your dreams – and in the never-fading memories with which I know you will always share with me.'

SIR DAVID TANG, on his 15-year-old West Highland Terrier, Hot

Lump had an absolutely pampered life there. Picasso once said, 'Lump, he's not a dog, he's not a little man, he's somebody else.' Picasso had many dogs, but Lump was the only one he took in his arms.

DAVID DOUGLAS DUNCAN, on Picasso and his dachshund Lump. Picasso died in April 1973, one week after the death of Lump

Not the least hard thing to bear when they go from us, these quiet friends, is that they carry away with them so many years of our own lives.

    JOHN GALSWORTHY, *Memories*

[One who] possessed beauty without vanity,
Strength without insolence,
Courage without ferocity,
and all the virtues of Man without his vices.

    LORD BYRON, eulogy to his Newfoundland Boatswain

Old Blue died and he died so hard,
Shook the ground in my back yard.
Dug him a grave with a silver spade,
Lowered him down with a golden chain.
Every link I did call his name.
Here Blue, you good dog you
Here Blue, I'm coming there too.

    JOAN BAEZ, traditional folk song

May all dogs that I have ever loved carry my coffin howl at the moonless sky,
and lie down with me sleeping when I die.

    ERICA JONG, "Best Friends" *At the Edge of the Body*

If there is no God for thee
Then there is no God for me.

    ANNA HEMPSTEAD BRANCH,
    "To A Dog" *Sonnets From a Lock Box*

From Trixie to Lulu and beyond, my dogs have guided me on a spiritual sojourn. They were fearless champions of faith – faith in each other, faith in the Great Spirit that lives in each of us. Lulu opened that final door for me, total openness and trust between God's creatures. Perhaps only dogs in their innocence can teach us that.

    BILL HENDERSON, *All My Dogs*

Well you can't shoot a church-goin' dog. It would be a sin.

    ANNA SOPHIA ROBB (Opal), in *Because of Winn-Dixie*

All dogs go to heaven because, unlike people, dogs are naturally good and loyal and kind.

    WHIPPET ANGEL, in *All Dogs Go To Heaven*

The dog is a gentleman; I hope to go to his heaven, not man's.

    MARK TWAIN

If I have any beliefs in immortality, it is that certain dogs I have known will go to heaven, and very, very few persons.

    JAMES THURBER

Marley's spirit is up in dog heaven right now. He's in a giant golden meadow, running free. And his hips are good again. And his hearing is back, and his eyesight is sharp, and he has all his teeth. He's back in his prime – chasing rabbits all day long.

    JOHN GROGAN, *Marley and Me*. Grogan is talking to his children about Marley's last day.

Heaven goes by favor; if it went by merit, you would stay out and your dog would go in.

MARK TWAIN

It is a terrible thing for an old lady to outlive her dogs.

TENNESSEE WILLIAMS, *Camino Real*

Dogs are our link to paradise.

MILAN KUNDERA

If there is a heaven, it's certain our animals are to be there. Their lives become so interwoven with our own, it would take more than an archangel to disentangle them.

PAM BROWN, Australian poet

"Do you think He made a place for dogs to hunt? You know – just like we have here on our place – with mountains and sycamore trees, rivers and cornfields, and old rail fences? Do you think He did?"
"From what I've read in the Good Book, Billy," she said. "He put far more things up there than we have here. Yes, I'm sure he did."

WILSON RAWLS, *Where the Red Fern Grows*

After he died there were a lot of nights when I was certain that I could feel him get into bed beside me and I would reach out and pat his head. The feeling was so real that I wrote a poem about it and how much it hurt to realize that he wasn't going to be there any more.

JIMMY STEWART, on his golden retriever Beau

My friendship with Mitzi was like the friendship that many children have with their pets. My mother and father thought it was "good for me" to have a dog for a companion. Well it was good for me, but it was only many years after she died that I began to understand how good it was, and why.

FRED ROGERS (Mr. Rogers)

One last request I earnestly make. I have heard my Mistress say, "When Blemie dies we must never have another dog. I love him so much I could never love another one." Now I would ask her, for love of me, to have another. It would be a poor tribute to my memory never to have a dog again. What I would like to feel is that, having once had me in the family, now she cannot live without a dog!

EUGENE O'NEILL, *Last Will and Testament of An Extremely Distinguished Dog*

A NOTE ON THE TYPE

The text of this book was set in Minion, a word that not only refers to a size of type but also is defined (appropriately enough) as "faithful companion." Minion was designed by Robert Slimbach for Adobe Systems in 1990. In Slimbach's own words, "I like to think of Minion as a synthesis of historical and contemporary elements. My intention with the design was to make a progressive Aldine style text family that is both stylistically distinctive and utilitarian. The design grew out of my formal calligraphy, written in the Aldine style. By adapting my hand lettering to the practical concerns of computer aided text typeface design, I hoped to design a fresh interpretation of a classical alphabet." The display face used for chapter openings is Linoscript designed by Morris Fuller Benton in 1905. Linoscript is reminisent of handwriting found in early twentieth century school books and diaries.

Book design by Sara Eisenman